Spend Time With Me:

A Story To Inspire

Transformational Leaders

RACHEL STONE

Published in 2024 by Discover Your Bounce Publishing

www.discoveryourbouncepublishing.com

978-1-914428-26-5

Page design and typesetting by Discover Your Bounce Publishing

DEDICATION

For Mum, Neil, Ian, Dawn, Lia, Joe, Luke, Laurie and Rudy, Edwin, Nan, Graham, Sandra, Sue S and my lovely, patient caring, supportive friends.

CONTENTS

FOREWORD
BY PROFESSOR DAMIAN HUGHES

There is a famous – possibly apocryphal - story about Pablo Picasso which I was reminded of, whilst reading Rachel's incredibly personal and extremely powerful book.

One day, Picasso welcomed a stranger into his studio. On the floor in the middle of the studio, he had a large lump of rock. The visitor asked Picasso what he intended to do with it. 'From that rock, I will sculpt a lion,' the great artist replied.

The visitor was taken aback. It's hard to imagine how anyone could create anything from such a rock. In obvious awe of Picasso, he asked the master nervously what, how, where one might start the process of creating a lion from such an unpromising block of stone.

'Oh, it's very simple,' Picasso replied. 'I just take my chisel and knock off all the bits that don't look like a lion.'

This engaging book is like sitting and listening to Rachel explain how she became a life-changing coach by removing all of the bits in her life that don't help and just keeping the bits that do.

I hope you will enjoy reading it as much as I have.

INTRODUCTION

"You've had an interesting life" people often say. I hope it continues to be so! I've learnt so much and it feels extremely important to share my learning. My mantra is always that it's not what happens to you that matters, but how you respond.

Like most people, I have had to respond to challenges, but for a while in my younger days I was stuck in a type of victim mode and felt that life was being unfair to me.

When the going got tough I transformed my mindset and changed my life.

It feels important that I share this story to help others do the same, especially those in leadership roles.

We are facing massive challenges as a species. It will require leaders to help us all.

Leaders around the globe urgently need to get on board with what is changing in the business world. *All coaches are leaders, but not all leaders are coaches.* This must change. The market is different. The younger generation of employees and consumers are done with the old ways. Work must appeal to the new emerging leaders in a way that inspires them.

Significantly, all leaders must carry out progression planning, and develop their replacements. That's why coaching skills are so important. The new blood coming up through the ranks will not be TOLD what to do, or 'obey' through transactional, old-fashioned 'command and control' methods. Out-of-date tactics, relying on fear and intimidation, are unacceptable. They also don't work with the new generation. Why would they?

Younger recruits are searching for meaning and purpose. Perhaps, more people are generally, too. We are facing challenging times. Transformational leadership is coming into its own.

So many senior people within organisations had to climb the corporate ladder the hard way. They were promoted without development or training. They often lack the insight or experience to coach.

It is paramount that leaders win hearts and minds to lead successfully at this pivotal point in business. Transformational leadership delivers a route to the new way of doing business, especially post-Covid.

The **Kindness Economy** is catching on. A big shout out to Mary Portas and her dedication to making this part of the business debates now taking shape. People, Planet and Profit matter – in that order.

Transformational leadership is the best way you change organisational culture. I wanted to write this book to inspire transformational leaders.

I have affected change in over 100 companies, coaching and training over 200 CEOs, MDs, senior managers and under-performing teams. My angle is that it is possible to create change by learning something new and then produce a ripple effect, which will change the way leaders lead and the way we all do business.

My approach is practical and do-able. I was just a normal ex-Safeway

Manager, stay-at-home mum who moved on through extremely challenging personal circumstances to become the main financial provider for her family as a Business Studies teacher. So disappointed with the poor leadership within the organisations I worked for, I *transformed* my life and found my purpose.

I want my legacy to be that others do the same. That's why I wrote this book.

This book tells my story and I share my learning, so that others can relate to transformational leadership and get straight on with doing it.

Most books in this field are purely academic, high-brow – only accessible to more intellectual types, CEOs of massive corporate concerns, not the majority of leaders in the SME sector. These smaller companies need to be developing and growing the headcount and moving people from 'doers' to 'leaders' for a secure future for thousands of young people leaving education.

My start in life was unconventional to say the least.

Part One is a true story, which starts in 1972 when my family goes away on holiday with the family next door. On returning from the two weeks in Wales, in two caravans, we drive back all jumbled up. I'm not with my dad, or my beloved brother, but in the car with my mum, the man from next door and his daughter. It all went wrong from there.

My parents married the couple next door and they shared the children. It was a disaster.

I grew up with zero self-worth, but embarked on a career in management. Getting to that point, aged 21, I had some challenges (and some brilliant times, too!), all of which helped shape me into, what

I thought, was a well-rounded person. What I didn't know at that point is that there is a huge difference between confidence and self-worth.

Getting married young seemed like the answer. I was desperately keen to raise a family, only I would do it properly... I met and married a lovely man.

It didn't go to plan. We experienced very trying times where I had to sacrifice my ideals and become the main financial provider for the family. I couldn't spend the time I wanted to as a stay-at-home mum.

With a sick husband, who lost his mum and his job in the same week, a one-year-old and a three-year-old, no family support to speak of and having to have a hysterectomy two weeks before, I started a degree course which included a PGCE, to become a Business Studies teacher.

Sorted. Or was it? That didn't go to plan either.

So, in 2012, from zero, I started my own business after a great deal of further learning and development.

Part Two captures my learning and experience and sets out how to become an effective transformational leader. I share the learnings and experience of the best ways to move people forward towards a goal. The 13 years I've spent coaching and training leaders has helped me build up a wealth of knowledge and experience, which is shared in an accessible way, both easy to read and apply.

As the world faces many crises, we look to leaders to shape the changes we need. Now, more than ever, we need leaders to inspire people to do the right things in the right way.

This book sets out to help leaders learn how.

PART ONE

CHAPTER ONE

1972, GOING ON HOLIDAYS WITH THE NEW NEXT-DOOR NEIGHBOURS

This is a true story.

I was five years old in the summer of 1972. It was a tense time in the UK, as Prime Minister Ted Heath declared a state of emergency due to the dockers' strike. The IRA campaign was at its peak, and newspapers worldwide were filled with stories of hijackings and bombings in Tel Aviv and the tragic Summer Olympics massacre in Munich.

Being blissfully unaware of all this, I was thrilled to discover we had new neighbours arriving next door. A family with two girls moved into 8 Drake Avenue. I lived at number 10. To my delight, Alison was the same age as me. Her sister, Dawn, was a couple of years older. We instantly became great friends. Their mum and dad were called Eddie and Irene.

Living with me at 10 Drake Avenue were my mum and dad (Kay and Rex) and my brother, Ian. He was ten and I worshipped him. In fact, legend has it that my first words were "My brother is at school". Apparently, I spent my time as a toddler waiting in the front garden for him to come home. Dad was a skilled builder and Mum helped him build the bungalow that year. It was a lovely home, always spotlessly clean and tidy.

Mum and Irene became great friends. Ten Drake Avenue was filled with laughter at the weekends, when all the grown-ups got together for fun evenings, playing cards, whilst all of us children played outside, usually up the street with bikes and footballs. We also had great times, especially when we were laughing in the field opposite, where we had fun flinging horses' poo with sticks we found lying around!

It's funny what stays in your mind. I noticed straight away how different my new friends' lives were at number 8. It struck me how cool it was that their shopping included peanuts and orange squash in great big pack sizes. I was impressed to hear about the huge chest freezer, in which they stored big tubs of ice cream in exotic flavours, such as raspberry ripple! They even had chocolate sauce to pour on top. We certainly didn't have those things at number 10.

Their two dogs were called Bella (the golden Labrador, who was gentle and cuddly) and Robbie (the Alsatian, who was slightly less so). Their dad, Eddie, always had black, greasy hands. He was a very good car mechanic. The driveway in front of number 8's garage was always filled with at least two random cars waiting to be fixed.

That's all I knew about number 8, I never went inside, neither did Mum, until after 'the swap'.

I'll explain.

All four of us kids screamed with excitement when we were told that both families were going away on holiday together, in our two cars, towing two caravans. We were thrilled!

I can only remember two things about that life-changing holiday. One being the journey back home. We came back in the same two cars, but we were all jumbled up. We weren't sitting how we did when we set off for the holiday.

The second one being that we had to spend a couple of days waiting for Dad to get better after he collapsed by the side of the road. We were in a big traffic jam. He got out of the car to have a wee, but didn't come back.

Ian was sent to look for Dad. He found him lying in the grass. He came running back screaming, "Dad is on the floor with his pants down!"

Dad had collapsed due to nervous exhaustion. He spent time resting in hospital before he was well enough to make the drive home. We all waited for him – staying in the two caravans in the hospital car park.

The four of us children had no idea what had been going on behind the scenes, but we were soon to find out.

As we set off home, I thought it was odd that I wasn't in our car with Dad and Ian. Mum and I were going home in Eddie's car with Alison. Ian was in Dad's car with Irene and Dawn. All very strange.

Then Mum turned her face back to me and Alison. She explained that when we arrived home, we would be living with her and Eddie, in Eddie's house, number 8. She went on to say that Ian would be living with Dad and Irene, in our old house (number 10). Dawn would be his 'new sister'.

I would be able to see Dad and Ian whenever I wanted, as they would only be next door, and Alison would be my 'new sister'. Alison could see her mum and Dawn as often as she wanted, as *they* would be just next door. I immediately started to cry. I wanted to be with my brother. I didn't want him to have a new sister. They stopped the car so that I could sit with him. I was confused.

We all got back at to Drake Avenue late that night.

The two caravans pulled up outside numbers 8 and 10. Alison and I were bundled into number 8. My new bedroom was small and cluttered and I was allowed to sleep in the top bunk.

CHAPTER TWO

LIVING NEXT DOOR

It was very strange and awkward following that initial rearranging of the two families. I think everyone felt uncomfortable in their unfamiliar surroundings. I know I did. I longed for *my* clean and tidy bedroom, along with all the things that used to belong to me and my 'proper family' – things that made it a home. Number 8 was so very different from number 10.

It's weird that I fixated on wanting to hold Mum's piggy bank, which was a 'special thing' she let me play with sometimes. It was a precious 21st birthday present she coveted and occasionally allowed me to handle. I used to beg for hours to be allowed to do so. When I went next door to see Dad, it was still there on the shelf. I thought Mum should have it with her, in the other house. I wondered, "Is it Irene's now?" That felt wrong, but I was too afraid to mention it. I wanted to hold it and touch the cool, smooth surface and to feel good about being allowed to have it again. Everyone looked angry most of the time, so I did not ask. 'Being good' suddenly felt *very* important.

Going next door to see Dad and Ian was odd. I liked being back in my nice-smelling number 10, my old home. Number 8 smelled of dogs. Things were different in number 10 now, things had moved. Other people's things were where my things had been.

Dawn was being a sister to *my* brother. She often told me, "Ian is my brother now". I hated it and I hated her for saying it. It made me want to cry. Holding that back, while trying to '*be good*' was very hard. It made my eyes sting and my throat tight. I would try to swallow the feeling down like a lump. Dad was in the background. I can't actually remember talking with him on any of those visits. I must have done, though. Surely?

I felt a sad ache most of the time. I missed being with my wonderful brother, and I wanted to go into his bedroom in the mornings and play the 'annoy Ian' game, like we used to when we both lived at number 10. I would beg and beg him to do 'push offs'. He would lay on his back with his knees squashed up to his chest. I would balance on the up-turned soles of his feet, and he would fling his legs out sending me flying. It made us laugh so much, especially if I fell off the bed. He used to pretend he didn't want to play and make me beg him to do it. Then he would let me think I had won.

The visits to see him were never as good as I hoped they would be. It wasn't the same anymore. Dawn was always there.

I was a bit shy of my new 'Uncle Eddie'. He was very different from Dad. Dad was quiet, stiff, smart, clean, tall, blonde and slim, whilst Eddie was funny, round in shape, spoke loudly and had messy, curly black hair. Eddie spent a lot of time fixing cars. The garage joined the house through a doorway in the hall, but we were not allowed in there. It was dark and smelled of oil (so did Eddie, and it bothered me that his hands were always dirty with black, greasy nails). I knew the garage was a dangerous place because Mum repeatedly warned us not to go in or to touch any of the car bits, which were strewn all around the house. He also had a collection of guns stored in the garage. He was a keen (and successful) clay pigeon shooting fan. That made me a little scared of Eddie, but I doubt that was justified. It was just strange and different.

Eddie talked a lot, made jokes and was always teasing us. He nicknamed me Squirt, because I was smaller than Alison. When Top of the Pops came on TV he would grab his out-of-tune acoustic guitar and pretend to play it, strumming randomly, whilst singing along to the Bay City Rollers, or Showaddywaddy! This was all so alien to me. I could hardly recall Dad speaking much, let alone singing.

Alison sat on Eddie's lap a lot, which was also new to me. There wasn't much lap-sitting in my old life, but I grew used to seeing it and wondered why Dad and me didn't do the same thing. Eddie cuddled Alison (and Mum) all the time. He often lifted her up, high above his head and swung her around. I'd never seen much cuddling before. When I visited Dad next door, I hoped he would swing me around like that, but he didn't.

Almost straight after 'the swap', Alison and I became very close, naturally just like sisters. I loved being with her. She was a tom boy and loved fishing and animals. Whereas I was a girly-girl who loved dolls and reading. I was much smaller than her, but a couple of months older. She was brave and strong and I was impressed by her messy, curly hair. She never brushed it and always created a fuss when it was bath or hair-wash time. At first, I never wanted to bath either, following her lead. Added to that, the bathroom was dirty, especially the first time I went in it. I was shocked by the grimy line around the bath – it was a grey/black colour (probably from the car oil, I realise now). I was horrified by it. So was Mum. She scrubbed it frantically with Ajax. There was no bubble bath, so we used 'Squeezy' washing-up liquid. The towels smelled and I wanted to go home to *my* nice bathroom with clean towels and proper bubble bath. And *my* bed.

Mum battled regularly with Alison to wipe her nose, or blow into a tissue, as she nearly always had dried-on bogies going crusty around her nostrils, which wound Mum up. She cried for her mum and Dawn. I tried to cheer her up. I could already read quite well by then. I did my best to read to her. Mum worried a lot when Alison was upset.

Number 8's back garden had loads of dog mess, which I found disgusting. I was not used to that! At Number 10 we had a gentle cat, Timmy (he was Ian's cat for sure, not mine). Getting used to dogs was tricky. Brave Alison was very happy to lie on top of either of them and boss them around. I was nervous of them and wished I could be brave like Alison. I was nervous quite a lot during those early days.

A short while into the new arrangements the bailiffs called at number 8.

Mum wasn't expecting that.

CHAPTER THREE
THEY MOVED AWAY – THEY MADE LEGAL HISTORY – TWO WEDDINGS

When the devastating news came that Ian, Dad, Irene and Dawn were moving from Drake Avenue, it hit me hard. It hit everyone hard. They weren't moving far away, but it was at the end of the world for me. I sat in the bedroom on moving day. I looked out of the window and saw my brother, who was crying his eyes out in the garden next door. I hid behind the curtain, crying too. I didn't want him to know I was upset and that I could see him. I thought he would be embarrassed about it. I wanted to go to him, but wasn't sure if I was allowed.

That was a difficult weekend.

After that, Mum and Eddie argued. I could hear them, because Eddie was loud. I wasn't used to that. I couldn't remember anything like that at home before 'the swap'.

It was tricky back at school. I tried to explain what had happened during the holidays.

I told my teacher, Miss Peck, "My mum and dad have swapped partners with the man and lady next door and I have a new sister. My brother lives next door now."

My favourite dinner lady cried when I told her my brother was moving away. I carried his photo with me in my school bag. I showed it to her every day. She kissed it, so I did too.

In October, Alison and I went to Ian's birthday party at his new house. He seemed happy, which was good. I was very sad saying goodbye, though.

In the half-term holiday, soon afterwards, Ian and his friend cycled the 15 miles (on main roads) to see Mum and me. I felt so important, because I was sure he really only came to see *me*. I was so proud he had done such a brave thing. It was brilliant to have time with him like that – no Dawn, Alison or Irene. He was only 11 years old! The grown-ups were furious. There was a huge row.

Then came a massive blow. Number 10 were moving to Lincoln. I didn't know where that was, but I found out that it was 250 miles away. I knew that was really far away, further than London, even. I couldn't bear it. It stung me right in my chest. I had just got used to the arrangements and settled with it as OK. Now it was going to be worse. The grown-ups promised we would still be able to visit. Us children would spend alternate school holidays at the two houses.

Meanwhile, Mum, Eddie, Alison and I also moved. We spent six months living in a caravan, while Mum and Eddie built a house. Granddad, Uncle Ed and Uncle Andrew (Mum's brothers) helped, too. It was cosy in the caravan with us four and the two dogs! Alison and I shared a single bed, sleeping top-to-toe.

We were only there for six months. Mum was very unhappy. When I was terribly sick for two whole days, following a trip to the dentist to have five of my back teeth out under anaesthetic, Mum called the doctor out. She was highly embarrassed about our living arrangements, so before he arrived, she hurriedly hid the evidence that us girls shared a bed.

In later years, Mum told me that while they were building the house, the two divorces taking place built a new precedent in law.

Apparently, both couples agreed to file for divorce on the grounds of adultery. It was much harder, back then. The courts were less willing to grant divorces. Each married couple took the advice of their appointed solicitors about how to handle this complex situation. The two cases were being heard one after the other on the same day.

Eddie and Irene went first. All went according to plan at that stage.

However, when Dad stood in the dock, he told a truthful account of the events leading up to the infamous caravan holiday. He accidentally informed the whole court room that he had 'given his wife permission to have sex with Eddie'. Evidently, he was *definitely not* supposed to say that.

The judge immediately halted the proceedings and renounced the decision he had made in his preceding case. The judge was astounded! Legal history was made with Dad's honest account of the shenanigans taking place in Drake Avenue during the heady days of summer 1972. Never had a divorce, which had just been granted, been suddenly revoked!

Following extensive faffing around with legal paperwork, all four newly divorced adults left the building, somewhat admonished by the judge.

How did they feel…?

17

Once our big, new house was finished, Mum and Eddie got married. There was no 'do'. I don't remember Dad marrying Irene, but they did get married. I saw the photo. No one mentioned it.

Between the ages of five and eleven, it was grim at times. There must have been some good days, but I can't recall many.

CHAPTER FOUR

FIGHTING OVER THE GIRLS AND ELVIS IS DEAD

A distinct feeling growing inside me was that I was not worth fighting over, and certainly not worth spending time with.

Both my stepsisters were obviously loved very much by both their parents. I knew this, because there were many arguments about where Dawn and Alison should live. Eddie and Irene fought over and about them. There was none of that over Ian and I.

I hated the school holidays. On the one hand, I would be able to see Ian, but on the other hand, if it was one of the holidays all four children would be in Lincoln with Dad and Irene, I would invariably have time on my own.

Irene was a good mum to Dawn and Alison. She lavished lots of time and energy on her girls. She didn't seem so keen on me. Why would she be? I wasn't her daughter.

I spent a great deal of time in Lincoln just *waiting*. Ian went out with his friends, naturally. Teenage Ian didn't want his little sister tagging along with him. I waited longingly for him, or Dad, to come in, hoping we would spend some time together.

On 16th August 1977, whilst waiting alone in the house, I heard the news on the radio that Elvis had died. I cried uncontrollably. I think now, that my grief was not for Elvis so much, but more for what used to be my family. I was lonely and wanted to feel part of something.

Sometimes, Dawn and Alison would gang up against me to pick a physical fight. They taunted me about Eddie's nickname for me (Squirt). I was a bit frightened of Dawn and we didn't get on so well. I felt that Alison was torn between the two of us. She tried to be kind, and even tried to teach me to box to defend myself.

Us three girls were allowed to go over the fields to the River Witham to swim. We went by ourselves, which thinking about it now, as a mother myself, seems terrifyingly irresponsible of Irene, but things were different back then. Kids played outside all day.

On the way back from our swim, Dawn started a fight. I threw her knickers in a puddle and she wasn't letting me get away with that! I wonder, now, what made me do it. How foolish of me. As she came at me, I flew into a rage. I went completely wild and pummelled her, good 'n proper. I think I won that fight.

Alison clapped and cheered.

Both girls were much stronger and surer of themselves than I was. They were good at gymnastics and I was rubbish at it, but I was better at reading and schoolwork.

Evening mealtimes in Lincoln were stressful for me. Irene always put peas on my plate, even though I couldn't bear to eat them. It was torture waiting for her to say I couldn't get down from the table until I had finished. I was always the last one there.

We did all go out together, which was OK if I didn't have a migraine. I suffered with these a great deal at this time. Blind spots and feeling sick, in addition to the pounding headache, made me feel like a wimp. I wanted to lie down in a dark room, but felt I had to be brave. Dad wasn't anywhere on the scene.

He had a teaching job at Lincoln College by this time, and with it being the school holidays, I suspect he was not at work but just out of the way. I can't be sure. There is just a blank where he should have been.

In late August 1978, Irene rang Eddie to tell him he had to have Dawn living with him. Dawn was being difficult and getting into trouble at school. This was 'breaking up' Dad and Irene's marriage, and there was the massive row on the phone that night.

From then on, the girls moved backwards and forwards between both parents at various times.

Ian told me years later that Dawn regularly tormented him and hit him, but he would never fight her, until one day, he couldn't hold it back any more and he did retaliate. He was severely punished. Dad lost his temper even more when Ian 'bad-mouthed' Mum. That was the trigger for Dawn to come to live with me, Eddie, Mum and Alison. So Ian was in Lincoln, with no sister.

I think now, as a mother myself, what must Dawn have been going through? What must those grown-ups have been feeling? What a mess…

The misery piled up further, when Dawn told Alison to stop calling my mum, 'Mum'. She was not Alison's mum. She was just 'Kay'.

Up until that point, Alison was happy to call her 'Mum'. Dawn said that Irene cried for Alison every night and Alison believed it, so she begged Eddie to go to Lincoln to be with her mum. I felt sorry for her.

I thought Dawn was bullying Alison, who became very unhappy. Eddie was furious and distraught. Sleepless nights followed, as Eddie and Irene fought on the phone over their girls again.

It made me think: 'Mum and Dad don't fight over me, or Ian. They don't love us as much.'

Christmas wasn't a happy time. Yes, all of us children got together, so I saw Ian, but the piles of presents were not equal. The Christmas tradition at both houses was that presents for each child were placed on individual chairs. Two chairs had huge piles of presents for Dawn and Alison on them. The other two chairs were not stacked so high.

Alison did move to Lincoln. Eddie was broken-hearted. He began to plan expensive holidays to give himself something to look forward to. He wanted to take his beloved girls somewhere nice. Dawn became an even more challenging teenager, and she seemed hell-bent on destroying Mum.

As an adult I look back on Dawn's outrageous behaviour and I realise that she was hurting. This reaction was her way of communicating about her anguish over the unsettling situation. However, it made life extremely miserable, especially for Mum. She could not cope, and was 'doped out of her head on Valium' (her words) for much of the time.

CHAPTER FIVE
LEAVING EDDIE ONCE, TWICE, THREE TIMES

Mum knew it wasn't sustainable to live this way. Eventually, we left Eddie. It took us three attempts to finally make the break.

Christmas 1977, at the end of the school holidays, Mum realised the situation wasn't working.

There was a massive build-up of tension. For the whole of that break, every night was filled with Eddie's voice booming along the hallway as he yelled at Mum. Repeating relentlessly, "Just say you love me! You will learn to mean it."

It was frightening. He was a big man and very powerful. I had never heard Dad shout. Ever. He hardly spoke, in fact – at least not to me.

As soon as Eddie went to work, we made our escape. In the bitter cold, with deep snow laying all around, we secretly left in Mum's friend's car. We went to Thanet to stay with Mum's parents, my nan and granddad.

Eddie came after us immediately, once he discovered we were gone. It was one of the scariest experiences of my life.

Shortly after arriving at Nan's, Mum and I popped to the village for some supplies. It was slow-going, due to the icy conditions. We had only gone as far as the next road along from Nan's when Eddie's red Jaguar sped towards us, skidding to a halt at a wonky angle, right up close to us.

He leapt out of the driver's seat and launched himself towards Mum. His face was red and angry. His matching red swollen eyes fixed intently on Mum. Tears streamed down his unshaven face. His wildly messy, curly black hair was almost upright. His lips looked blue.

He shouted angrily, "Get in the car!" totally unaware I was there.

He flung his arms around Mum, grabbing at her thick coat, whilst trying to drag her into the car.

She instinctively reached out to cling on to the garden wall to the side of her.

"Go and fetch Granddad!" she screamed to me, so I ran off as best I could on the ice. I didn't really want to leave her, but I knew I had to get help.

As I turned away to leave, I saw one of Eddie's guns on the back seat of the car.

By the time I reached Nan's, I was hysterical. I managed to blurt out: "Eddie's got Mum and he's got a gun in the car!"

They hurriedly took me to their neighbour and rushed off. Uncle Andrew was summoned to join them as back up.

Eddie was never going to shoot us, but I didn't know that at the time. He was desperate. He had lost Alison and thought he was losing Mum.

Eddie drove us home that night. I was reluctant to go, but Nan reassured me. She gave me the biggest, tightest hug I'd ever had.

I prayed all night to 'forgive and forget'. I was very religious at the time. I found God at school and focused on that to give me comfort. I prayed to be able to clear the image of Eddie's face as he got out of the car. It did work.

Dawn was sent back to Lincoln. We continued to have alternate holidays at either house.

Although I wasn't very close to my dad's mum, she was still quite significant in my life up to that point. We did visit her from time to time, before 'the swap'.

Dad did something unusual mid-way through the holiday: he called me upstairs to his bedroom. He gestured for me to sit on his bed. Interested and excited about what might be happening, I waited patiently whilst he arranged his photography kit. (He was a keen member of the photography group, apparently.) Without turning around to face me, he announced: "By the way, Nanny Tanner's dead."

"Oh. That's sad," I replied.

He continued to fiddle with cameras. I remained sitting there, watching the back of him.

Eventually he said, "You'd better go down."

I'm pretty sure he was upset, but I couldn't see his front.

That was my last ever school holiday in Lincoln.

I stopped going just to be ignored and went to stay with my nan instead. It occurred to me that I should visit her in case she died, too.

It upset me not to see Ian, but I had to make the break. I was 11 by this time and knew that I needed not to be there. It was hard explaining to Dad on the phone why I didn't want to go. He didn't try to talk me out of it. I said I thought Irene would be pleased.

I hung up the phone then locked myself in the toilet and cried for hours. I wanted him to beg me to continue visiting him. He didn't.

Despite Eddie's promise to Mum, that she would never have to look after his girls again, he tried to convince Mum to have them to live with us. It caused a great deal of tension and misery every day for two years. He had made this promise so that Mum would agree to come back to him, but he never meant it. As soon as we got home after the gun in the car incident, he said, "Now I'm getting my girls back."

In the summer of 1978, with football mania for the Argentinian World Cup at fever pitch, Mum decided to make another break for it. We ran away to London to stay with Mum's aunt, Granddad's youngest sister, Betty. She lived in Wimbledon, and Eddie couldn't find us. I missed the end of the school summer term. Mum and I had a wonderful six weeks, and it was great! We were so close to the Wimbledon Championships, although we didn't go. However, we loved having strawberries and cream, and idolised Bjorn Borg on the tiny, black and white TV. Great Aunty Betty was a fabulous cook, and we had the time of our lives with her.

Despite the promise Mum made to me ("We are never going back, Rach") she agreed to give Eddie another chance. I was gobsmacked.

Mum's friend told her that Eddie had attempted to take his own life. Both Mum's and Eddie's friends tried to reconcile them.

We went back. The summer holidays were nearly over. Mum, Eddie and I went camping in the New Forest. Just us three. I was numb. Mum was quiet, whilst Eddie was on his best behaviour.

The reconciliation did not last long. It rapidly deteriorated into a hellish experience. By November, Mum was planning another escape.

Mum told me, secretly, to leave a few vital belongings in the bottom drawer of my dressing table. She said I would go to school as normal. She would collect me when she was ready to make a run for it. She didn't know when, but I would know it was time, because I would get a signal in the form of a message from my teacher. The teacher would tell me, "The balloon has gone up."

Sure enough, halfway through a home economics lesson, the following week, the teacher relayed the message. I told her that I had to meet Mum in reception, as we were 'running away'.

I had the rest of that term off school. I spent a wonderful time helping Nan in her florist shop in Thanet. This was heavenly. We formed a wonderful bond. She saved me. I loved her totally and utterly. *She wanted to spend time with me.*

After the Christmas holidays, Mum and I commuted to our daily lives. This was a bit of a drag. Two trains (Birchington to Sheerness, changing at Sittingbourne) and two long walks to train stations at each end. We had some temporary accommodation in a nearly finished house, which Granddad was still building. Each morning at 5.30am we had breakfast with Granddad's friend, who lived next door to the building site, before walking to the train station. I would get out at Queenborough and meet friends. After school, I would walk to Mum's work, wait for her and we would commute home together, eat with Nan and Granddad, return to the unfinished house and go to bed.

Mum had her name down on a waiting list for a place for us to live through her work. It took a couple of months.

Eddie didn't come after us this time.

CHAPTER SIX

OUR PROPER LIVES

Aged 13, I was living with Mum in our own little flat, near to Mum's work, three miles from my school. We were incredibly hard up, but we began what I called 'our proper lives'. We were always good friends, but she wasn't a mother in the traditional sense. She went on, what I now know, was a self-destruct 'bender' of finding someone to love her. It was another phase of confusion as she had quite a few boyfriends, but there didn't seem to be any love there. I decided that this was not the way to have relationships. I grew up quickly and became very independent.

All the while I yearned for Dad to want to spend time with me. It hurt. He had made his life with Irene and was determined to make that a success, at the expense of his own children. He told me that on the phone. We planned a few visits to the little flat in Sheerness. They were mostly cancelled at the last minute. He visited his sister, who lived 20 miles away, but didn't come to see me.

I was obviously not worth spending time with.

I found out many years later that during this period, when Ian lived in Lincoln with Dad and Irene, Dawn and Alison, he was tragically unhappy. I'm glad I never knew that at the time.

My relationship with Dad (and his 'good lady wife') broke down further.

Mum and I made a few trips to Lincoln to visit Ian, and they were always fraught with tension. Irene always made it difficult for Ian, even though he had his own place by then, and she always made a scene on any visits. She would quiz him weeks before and for days afterwards. It caused him stress and that made us feel bad about visiting.

I began to wonder what Dad saw in Irene. From my experience, she wasn't that nice.

On the rare occasions I spoke to Dad, if I dared to ask about Irene, he always fiercely protected his 'good lady wife'. I hated it when he used those words. She made Ian and I miserable and I couldn't see anything much 'good' about her.

In 1981, when Mum turned 40, she met an angel in disguise – Charlie, who was 20 years her senior. I loved him dearly, as the father figure I never had, and we became great friends. He was a true *gentle*man in every sense. One Christmas I found a beautiful Christmas card which read, "To my wonderful friend this Christmas time". It was so apt. He laughed as he opened the envelope. He passed his one to me. On opening the envelope, I discovered he had chosen the exact same one for me!

Mum was very fond of him. He was a stable influence in our lives, and we had seven wonderfully happy years with him playing a major part.

In 1988, Charlie asked Mum to marry him, but she declined. She thought it wouldn't work. She didn't feel enough for him, it wasn't a mutual love. So she finished it with him. (RIP Charlie Nash. He died a year later of a brain tumour. Her biggest fear was that she wasn't in love with him enough to care for him as he got into his dotage. He suffered three heart attacks during the seven years they were a pair.) I still think of Charlie fondly when a song or a TV programme or any other reminder throws me back to the laughter and comfort we experienced having him around. He loved the song *The Power of Love* by Jennifer Rush. He would ask me to play it on the record player and whirl Mum around in the living room. When I hear it now I still recall the cheeky grin beaming all over his face, and remember how he would slip his hand down towards her bum. "*Charles!*" Mum would say, in a fake reprimand. "Rachel's here!"

Happy times.

School was the best part of my life. I loved it. I had lots of great friends. Mum was away most weekends at Charlie's, and I was totally independent. She would go off to work Friday mornings at 8am and I wouldn't see her again until she got back home from work Monday evening.

Sarah, one of my best friends, lived opposite me in a lovely posh house. She came to sleep over and we played 'Flats', making out we were sophisticated women of the world.

All our friends came to mine to hang out for the weekend. We had a brilliant time, and I was totally a mother hen to everyone. Three years in a row I hosted a daytime Christmas Eve party in that tiny little flat. Everyone got a little merry. It was all harmless fun. Not an adult in sight.

Mum trusted me to behave and not do anything stupid and I lived up to that trust. My friends respected the space and the freedom, and we were all really rather sensible! We had the most amazing friendship group, and I treasure the memories we created. I still have many close friends in my life originating from those happy times. I am blessed.

Thinking back on those fun-filled weekends without much adult supervision, between the ages of 13 and 16, I think that Mum played a highly risky strategy. It could have all gone terribly wrong. However, I didn't want to betray her trust. I remember that feeling of being trusted – I thrived on it. I thought about it a great deal when I had my own children (I also learnt the significant part trust plays in all relationships and organisations. More on that in Part Two).

I always tried to *be good*.

I was fairly happy with my O-Levels. I came away from 'the Comp' with seven good ones. The Sheppey Comprehensive did its best for me, and I did my best for it. That year, only 7% of my cohort achieved five or more O-levels at C grade or higher.

I made the break with 'the Comp' and chose to study science A-Levels at Mid Kent College of Higher Education, at the Horsted site in Chatham.

There were several factors in my choice:

- Mum said "Girls don't do science, you should do English and History". I had to do the complete opposite, *obviously!*

- I absolutely *loved* Physics and Chemistry.

- I didn't realise I would have to do Maths A-Level – what a bummer!

- I thought that by going to a bigger college, which meant I had to travel by train to get there every day, I would be preparing myself for the world of work.

- I knew that the most gorgeous hunk in the whole of 'the Comp' went there the year before me. My first love, Arron had blown me out, so I wanted a fresh new start.

- My dad had studied brickwork at the same college.

- My granddad taught brickwork at the college – that is how my mum met my dad.

I was one of only four girls in the Physics class. Sam, Sharon, Nymphia and I formed a united front, making friends quickly, especially Sam and I. She was much more of a boffin than me. I was the only one there with a lowly grade C (all the others had A grades). I was definitely the only one with a Grade 1 CSE (Certificate in Secondary Education). These qualifications had just been introduced. It was the forerunner to the GCSE, which replaced the O-Levels soon after. The teacher said it was a good back-up plan for me to do both.

I can proudly say now that I have Grade 1 CSE, Grade C at O-Level, and Grade E at A-level in Physics. So, my original plan to become a Research Scientist was blown!

CHAPTER SEVEN

TWO BRILLIANT WEEKS

I started my A-Levels in September 1985. I knew one person at that college and he didn't even know I existed! Mark Whitton – the most popular heart-throb at 'the Comp'. He was a year above me and was the superstar football player with actual fans and actual fan mail. By the November of that term, we were going out. I could not believe it!

Granddad was chuffed to bits I was attending 'his' college. He said, "I used to play bridge in the staff room at lunch times – we were quite serious players. My best opponent was a chap called Dr Lewis."

What a small world! He was only the head of my course and taught me three times a week. I couldn't wait to find out if he remembered Granddad (Arthur Clark). Of course he did!

"Your granddad was a very highly respected member of this college. He met Prince Phillip, you know! Great bridge player – brilliant teacher," Dr Lewis reminisced. He paused a while. I waited, because I thought he was going to say something important. "He was always good if you wanted freshly-laid eggs. His van was full of them…"

I was a bit disappointed. But then he added, "He used to give one of our lads a lift to and from college. A handsome, tall, blonde chap…"

And there you go. *Dr Lewis was talking about my dad.*

"That chap was my dad – Rex Tanner, Dr Lewis," I said, grinning from ear to ear.

"Oh, really! He was an excellent student, you know. One of our best at that time. He won us a few prizes in the bricklaying competitions!"

Funny how things pan out.

A little side note here about my granddad. During World War II, he was a sergeant in the Bomb Disposal Squad. A totally brave hero. So much so, in fact, that he was awarded the British Empire Medal for diffusing a massive, unexploded bomb, which landed on the Cardiff telephone exchange on 3rd March 1941.

Prince Phillip visited the college in the 1960s to open a new faculty. No doubt well prepared and briefed accordingly, Prince Phillip made a point of mentioning Granddad's Military Service Record. In the photo of that momentous occasion, Arthur Clark shook Prince Phillip's hand, proudly puffing out his chest.

Granddad had his faults, but he was certainly a very brave man.

Dr Lewis looked out for me because I was Arthur's and Rex's flesh and blood. I'm not saying I was a teacher's pet, but without his extra interest in my achievements, I would never have scraped through college like I did.

Despite that extra care, my attendance was shockingly bad in the second year. I wasn't aware of it then, that I was undoubtedly experiencing bouts of depression. My self-esteem was at rock bottom (but I didn't know it was called that, I just felt like shit). I cried most of the way through my Maths lessons, totally unable to focus and without a shred of any self-confidence in my ability. I didn't even like myself much.

I was on the wrong course. I should have been doing A-Level English and History and something else to fill up the programme... *Just like Mum said.*

Mum could see I was sliding downhill and took direct action. She paid for me to have a holiday, which turned out to be a fabulous experience. It definitely cheered me up at the end of that incredibly difficult first year of A-Level study.

I'd seen an advert for a college trip to the French Alps. It was rather expensive, but mentioned it to Mum, who said I should go and she would pay. That was a huge deal for her as money was *very* tight. I signed up straight away, not knowing what 'high altitude walking' involved. I was over the moon to be doing something new, whatever it was.

It turned out to be two of the best weeks of my life!

Mum dropped me off at college to join the huddle of teenagers gathering at the meeting point. She thanked the organisers profusely, adding emphatically, "I'm so grateful. I can have two whole weeks with no worries about her at all."

I never heard her say this, but the Group Leader, Mike Coyd, mentioned it to me later during the holiday. He asked me about my relationship with Mum. I said, "It's not your typical mum/daughter relationship. Why do you ask?"

"When I met your mum, she was so excited *for herself*, not excited about *your holiday*. I felt she was literally handing *you* over to *me*," he explained.

I shrugged my shoulders. I didn't know what to say.

Meanwhile, back on departure day...

Sixteen students and two tutors squeezed into two mini-buses with all the camping and climbing gear. Two of my Physics besties came too – Sam and Sharon. We had a blast!

We camped in the forest, by the river, in Argentiére, near Chamonix.

Then we climbed a mountain! Petite Aiguillee Verte, 3512m high. We stayed the night in a hut on the glacier, in a cramped dormitory, having made it there by climbing with crampons on our boots and ice picks in our hands. What an experience!

The walk across the glacier at 4am the next morning, with us all tied together by rope, wearing lamps on our heads, avoiding the crevices and admiring the view, was worth the slight altitude sickness and aching limbs. It was absolutely awesome. The majesty of the view totally blew my mind.

For the rest of the break, we walked around the Alps more sedately. Each night, huddled around a glowing fire, we sang along to Meat Loaf's classic album someone brought with them on cassette. *Bat Out of Hell* boomed out as loudly as we could on our battery-operated ghetto blaster. We thrashed that cassette tape to within an inch of its life every night until the batteries died!

Mike, the Group Leader, set us challenges each night to keep us all entertained. My favourite one of these was the spaghetti Bolognese competition. Each group had to make a delicious spaghetti Bolognese, which was awarded points for flavour, appearance, consistency and ingenuity, with no prior warning. None of us had the correct ingredients to hand, but Mike had a box of random food items we could select from once he gave the signal. He blew his whistle and there was a frantic scramble. It was hilarious that we all battled so competitively, pushing and shoving like those people on TV who had queued most of Christmas Day for the sale bargains on offer in Harrods on Boxing Day.

Sam, Sharon and I managed to grab a tin of corned beef, a tin of peas and a tin of spaghetti hoops. We didn't win, but we ate it! All that fresh air and walking miles made us ravenous all day, every day.

Mike was such a key part of the whole experience. What a great guy.

He ended every evening's fun singing his fabulous acapella rendition of the American folk song *Rock Island Line*, made famous by Lonnie Donegan. I'll never forget that 'Ol' pig iron!' It makes me cry happy tears to think back to that trip.

Another wonderful part of my life during these years was spending time with my long-term boyfriend, Mark, and his family, from when I was 16 up to turning 20. He was such a gorgeous, shy, kind and caring young man. His mum and dad made me feel like part of their family. When not at college, I was either at his house with him/them, or he was at the flat with me. Thanks to Mark Whitton, his parents, Ann and Dave, and his brother Gary, for bringing some normality into my life. *They made me feel loved and worth spending time with.* Truly special people.

I finished my A-Levels with an E in Physics, a D in Chemistry, and as for Maths... Well, at least I stayed the course, and was done with college... or so I thought.

CHAPTER EIGHT
STARTING WORK – AND THE INTER-RAIL
DISASTER

In 1987, despite rubbish A-Level results, I struck lucky when I joined the GEC Avionics Commercial Management Training Programme at the last minute. I squeezed on to the last place of that brilliant programme.

Mark and I flew back from a break in Tenerife. I got off the plane onto the train and went straight from Gatwick to Rochester to join the intensive induction programme.

I was rather disgruntled that I would have to spend Fridays at the college I thought I had just left! The programme included a day-release college course – BTEC HNC Business Studies. It was a fantastic learning experience, filled with group work, presentations, research and much more. That was the start of my passion for life-long learning and personal development. A flame was ignited, which still burns brightly to this day!

I absolutely loved every minute of it (except for the homework, of which there was loads!).

It was such a bonus that I did this course – it came in handy later on…

In work, I was lucky enough to experience every department and every aspect of that highly successful, global, world-leading manufacturing company.

I smashed the programme, loving every minute of my working life! What a brilliant opportunity. I learnt *so* much about people, processes, quality, standards, trade, customer service, cost control and more.

Leaving home was the natural next step. I took up lodgings just a mile from work. Mum was thrilled. My wages just covered my living expenses!

In 1989, on successful completion of the programme, I secured a job as an Assistant Buyer in the prestigious Airborne Display Division. The factory produced specialist F-16 Fighter Pilot helmets. My money went up – hurrah!

On my first day in my new job, I was set the task of expediting the production purchases to ensure crucial parts for production were delivered on time. I took this extremely seriously, knowing that a big team of production assistants would be standing idle without their components to assemble and that would be an expensive delay!

Most of the orders were for electrical parts linked to complex communication systems, so I thought nothing of phoning the Motorola Sales department to chase up the 'carriage charge'. I thought, "At least my Physics A-Level didn't go completely to waste. I'm working with scientific technology after all."

I was so embarrassed when I discovered that what I thought was a missing electrical component was actually *the cost for the delivery*. 'Carriage charge', oh blimey.

The guys in the office teased me for days afterwards. The early morning meetings started with Phil, the Production Manager, checking with me to see if the 'carriage charge' had arrived yet.

At least I was being thorough.

During the year that ensued, my desire to be part of building military weapons dwindled. I was becoming more politically aware, and I felt uncomfortable telling people where I worked.

I left for a promotion to become Office Manager and Buyer at Sandvik Coromant UK. My money went up – hurrah again! Another manufacturing firm – still global, but not on the same scale – based in a small production unit. I had my own small team to manage, and I blossomed into my new people-focused role.

I didn't escape being teased there, either. When our typist, Linda, went on holiday, I covered her work, the bulk of which meant I had loads of Purchase Order Requisitions to process. This entailed typing up the order, copying details from the handwritten slips Terry brought over from the warehouse each day.

One such slip was for 100 boxes of tiny diamond-tipped inserts for the cutting tools in the machine shop. These tips were called 'caps'. I was stitched up like a kipper by Terry, to see whether he could make me blush. I was unaware that a 'Dutch cap' was a name for a type of contraceptive. I was young and naïve!

I typed out exactly what he had written on the slip, not noticing the smiley face on the bottom next to his scrawly handwriting.

The Purchase Order was prepared in triplicate, one for Linda's file, one for Terry's goods-in office and one to the supplier, which was duly sent out in the post. I never thought any more of it.

One hundred Boxes of 'Dutch caps' – the diamond tipped variety – were on order as required. Job done. The Dutch bit was superfluous and on the slip for comedic purposes only. But I didn't know that.

Terry could not wait to announce on the Tanoy system – which was fed to every workspace on site – exactly what was on order, much to the amusement of everyone at work that day!

The supplier rang Terry to have a good laugh, too.

It's embarrassing to admit, here, that this wasn't the first time I had been stitched up like a kipper. I fell for one of the oldest gags in work prank history.

On my first day at Sandvik's, when I was as keen as mustard to make a good impression, my induction included spending time with the guys in the drawing office. They played a blinder! The office was almost completely filled by three huge drawing desks, all with massive sheets of specialist drawing paper, which were being held flat tightly by a kind of string, secured by a special sort of paperweight. This was to prevent the corners curling up. Pete, the Drawing Office Deputy Manager, showed me around, explaining everything that went on in his department. I listened, intently, to every word he said. He started fussing with the line of string one side of the drawings for his current project. Something wasn't right, apparently.

"This one isn't heavy enough," he explained. "Would you mind going to see Terry in the Stores for me?"

"Sure. What d'you need?" I responded, eager to please.

"Ask him to give you a ***long wait.***"

I should have been able to spot the smirk he must have been desperately trying to conceal as I trotted off enthusiastically.

Classic.

Despite being the butt of a few jokes, I grew massively in

confidence and worked really hard, because I loved my job and I loved working with the team.

There was much more flexibility in a smaller firm. Allowing me to spread my wings on projects and opportunities, which served me well further along my career path. At least I was working in a market which wasn't part of the instruments of war. A need to be true to my values was developing strongly within me.

That deep-rooted feeling of being true was the reason I knew I had to split up with Mark. I wasn't really being honest about my feelings. I knew deep inside that I loved being with his family as a whole, not necessarily being with him, and it wasn't fair.

So, I ended our lovely, four-year long relationship. It was a massive wrench to leave all that security behind, but it was for the best. It was a terribly difficult thing to do, because there was nothing bad going on. It was so good for me be *part of a family*, but it wasn't fair on Mark. That wasn't the right reason to be with him.

I didn't realise how unbalanced it would make me to turn my back on that security, and I become rather unsettled.

I felt terrible about breaking his heart and needed something to throw myself into.

Rather abruptly, I decided to go travelling around Europe using the popular Inter-Rail Card. It was all the rage at the time (no such thing as EasyJet back then!). The card gave travellers access to the entire European rail network at massively discounted prices.

Off I went. Backpacking with my friend Lisa, whom I'd met at GEC Avionics. We bonded in the day-release classes, often choosing to complete projects together. She was completely different from me and

I loved that. Her creativity impressed me.

We also had family stuff in common. Joining GEC Avionics led Lisa to discover she had a half-sister (the same age) working in the accounts department! Neither Lisa, or her mum, knew a thing about this until Lisa collected her wage packet one week (yes, we were paid in cash every week).

That day, while Lisa was being handed the small, brown envelope, the office assistant unexpectedly said, "I know you. You're my sister." It all unravelled from there. Another family with clandestine activities and extramarital affairs. Lisa didn't know whether to be pleased to have another sister, or devastated that her dad had betrayed her mum.

Parents, hey? Who'd have 'em?

So, in a rash move, we both packed in our jobs to travel the world, much to the dismay of both our mums.

Mum said, "Don't tell me, Rachel. I don't want to know." We didn't speak for weeks.

Lisa's mum said, "You'll be better off out of it for a while, it's going to get messy."

Off we went travelling. We were going to see the world! We heard that Venice was sinking, so we had better get there before it did!

We started our adventure sightseeing in Paris for a couple of days. Our plan was to do the south of France next. From Paris, we headed to Monte Carlo. By the time we arrived, though, a big, painful lump had appeared between my legs, and I felt rough. I hobbled around whilst we gawped at the super yachts in the marina. I desperately did not want to spoil the experience for Lisa.

Next, we took the overnight train to Rome – immediately *not* sticking to our plan!

I told Lisa I wasn't feeling great.

When the train pulled in early that morning, we hurriedly found a *pensione* and I got straight in bed, where I thought I would stay for just the day, to recover. I felt rotten having had no sleep. Searing pains were shooting through the core of me. I urgently needed to see a doctor.

Lisa went out sightseeing to give me the space to rest.

While she was gone, I went to reception to ask for help to make an appointment with a doctor. I was feeling much worse.

Luckily, the friendly, English-speaking hotel manager's son was on duty, because I promptly collapsed. He quickly and kindly arranged a taxi to take me to hospital. He told the driver something vague about 'female problems'. I wasn't able to speak much, as I was doubled-over in pain, sweating and being sick. I barely managed to point in the general direction of my painful area.

I was seen very quickly and in surgery by the end of the day. A small crowd of students and doctors were in the room, but frankly, I didn't care, as long as somebody did something to relieve the pain. A procedure to exorcise the cyst (which, by this point, was the size of a small melon) took place under local anaesthetic. I was then pumped full of antibiotics by injection every few hours. Apparently, this kind of cyst was fairly rare. Hence the on-lookers.

I felt physically loads better, almost immediately, and was frantic to tell Lisa where I was. There was nobody available in the hospital who could speak English for two more days…

Meanwhile, Lisa had come back to our hotel and I was nowhere to be seen. She didn't know where I was, until the hotel manager's son came back on duty, *three days* later! We didn't have mobile phones in those days. At this time, the news was full of Terry Waite's hostage situation. As I began to feel better, I thought about how dreadful it must be for him. I lay there wondering if Lisa would find me, and was she OK? Would I ever see a familiar face again?!

I'm not saying I was comparing my experience to Terry Waite's awful ordeal, but it certainly made me appreciate the value of being in familiar surroundings, connected to friends and family. What *must* it have been like for *him*?

At the end of the third day, a nurse came in and ran me a bath, whilst another nurse came in and gestured for me to get in it, which I did. The first nurse held me securely by the shoulders and the second one helped herself to the copious amounts of packing, which unbeknown to me, had been tightly stuffed into a small hole in the side of my vagina. I tried hard not to fight them off, or to scream out in pain. I wanted some of my dignity to remain intact. As soon as it was all removed, I was allowed out of the bath. I burst into tears and cried out as loud as I could, "*I just want to speak to someone in English! Pleeeeeeeease!*" I was quivering with shock.

"OK! OK! OK!" they said, scurrying off.

And sure enough, a couple of hours later, a lovely Maltese man appeared. He was dressed very smartly in a white tunic and black trousers. I thought he was a chef and I would be ordering a lovely supper! But, no. In perfect English, with a strong Maltese accent, he gently explained what had happened. He said that I should go home to England to see a gynaecologist as soon as I could. I thanked him and asked him to thank all the staff for looking after me. He hugged me, telling me "everything will be OK". I didn't know how he knew it, but I believed him. I never asked what his job was. He remains a mystery!

And then, as if by magic, Lisa appeared at the doorway. What a relief! The lovely hotel manager's son told Lisa what had happened and where she could find me. She came immediately. We laughed at how our adventure had not met our expectations.

We went back to our lovely, friendly, little hotel and went to bed. We discussed what we should do next. It was agreed that I would fly home the next day, courtesy of my travel insurance. Thank goodness I had the sense to get some!

Lisa wanted to go home, too. Her insurance wouldn't pay for her to fly, so she said she would get the train back to the ferry and go on home from there. She had to wait a day. We knew there was a train strike on. It was all over the news at the time. You couldn't miss it. Not great for those tourists with a Rail Card!

That night, around 11.30pm, as we chatted, lazily, laughing about how our 'travelling the world' adventure had all gone wrong, we were rudely interrupted by the piercing shrieks of the fire alarm.

We sat upright poised to take flight. For a very brief moment, we wondered whether it was a drill. We listened for clues, but heard a hullabaloo in the corridor. There was a loud knock at the door and people shouting. No, it wasn't a drill. There was actually a small, but real, fire in the hotel and we had to evacuate.

You couldn't make it up!

We followed the instructions and stayed outside, in the town square, with all the other guests. Everyone chatted about how lucky we had been that it wasn't more serious.

We were allowed back to our rooms around 5.30am.

I packed my things to fly home. The hotel manager allowed me to use the hotel phone, and thanks to the magnificent service provided by an organisation called STS Travel, I was booked on a flight later that same afternoon. If I remember correctly, STS was a specialist student travel organisation, popular at the time. I was guided to them by my insurance company, and it was a massive relief.

Lisa made plans to carry on sightseeing until she could take a train to the ferry.

In all the hubbub and the goings-on, Lisa made a tiny, little mistake when she phoned home from the phone box. She told her boyfriend, Dave, she was on her way back. She was a little tearful, having spent the last three days roaming around Rome alone, followed by a potentially life-threatening incident in the hotel, and she accidentally told him the wrong ferry journey time, by the not insignificant amount of *twelve hours*! He was dutifully there to meet her at the ferry terminal, waiting anxiously, because he knew Lisa was upset.

However, her incorrect instructions got him there a full twelve hours *before she would actually* arrive. When she failed to turn up, he called the police.

In 1976, the infamous serial killer Charles Sobhraj was jailed for mercilessly killing travellers exploring Asia. This undoubtedly made people, including Dave, more wary about the potential threats to young female tourists.

Lisa failing to arrive 'on time' caused a bit of a hoo-ha at the ferry terminal. There was hell to pay when she finally arrived!

That was the end of our travelling the world adventure! We had planned to work abroad, going from job to job, travelling by train, seeing the sights, making friends and, possibly, even picking up a bit of the lingo if we could. Oh well! At least we did get back safely.

CHAPTER NINE
THEY MOVED TO FRANCE

In 1989, Mum decided to move to France to live with Nan and Granddad, who had recently retired to the beautiful Lot et Garonne region in the south west of France. Granddad wanted to build a home in the picturesque village, where they had spent happy times during their many adventures in Europe after the war. He bought a superb plot of land with a fabulous view, and they set about it. He was 67 and she was 65. Incredibly courageous of them, especially as neither spoke the language.

I never knew Mum was depressed at that time. We didn't speak much then. It was a time in our lives when we were quite distant. I was angry with her. I'd left home at 18 to be independent, so she was free of responsibility. As Europe would be opening up in 1992 and there would be more international trade, she could find a good job, if her French speaking skills improved (she spoke fairly good French from her O-Level pass). She thought it might be a temporary thing. She ended up staying for 25 years.

She had a brilliant time, but she wasn't really in my life.

I felt that I wasn't worth spending time with.

CHAPTER TEN

WORK, MARRIAGE AND CHILDREN –
CHALLENGES COMING THICK AND FAST

By the end of 1989, I wanted more of a challenge at work. I thought I might have good people skills, because I had been told this many times. On arriving back from the disastrous 'travelling the world' project, I moved in with Pete – the chap from the drawing office with a good sense of humour! He kindly came to pick me up from the airport. We had been dating a bit, and it seemed like a good idea to live together. I think I lurched into that decision without a lot of thought.

I temporarily took an early morning cleaning job at the primary school at the end of Pete's road, sold jewellery in the evenings and worked during the day at Marden Fruit Packers. The packing crew mainly consisted of people from the local Traveller community. It was a great experience, quite physically demanding and not at all cerebral, but I learnt so much about motivation and mechanisation. The supervisor used great techniques to keep everyone on task.

It wasn't great career progression, but it gave me some income.

It turned out I was great at selling jewellery! I did so well that I won an award and was invited to the region's celebration evening. I was reluctant to go up on stage, because in the rush to get ready, I didn't notice that I had accidentally put odd shoes on. I made a joke of it and said I'd done it on purpose – I didn't get away with that!

Around this time, I thought it was time to get serious about a career.

The next morning, I scoured the newspaper for a suitable job vacancy with good prospects. I found an advert for the Safeway Retail Management Training Programme, which appealed to me because it emphasised teamwork. I applied and was successful. Aged 21, I completed the nine-month long Senior Management Programme with flying colours. It was a superb training experience.

I was appointed Assistant Manager, Seaford Branch. (£500,000 turnover a week, 250 staff and 50,000 product lines. I loved it!)

At this point I was an extremely confident 21-year-old woman. However, I was soon to discover that I had incredibly low self-worth. Depression hit me when Mum left for France and I moved to East Sussex for my work. I worked every hour I could, and Pete and I split up. I felt alone. But not for long…

Luckily for me, a year later, I fell in love with a lovely man, Neil Stone, and became blissfully happy. For the first time in my life, I think I felt truly secure. We met at Safeway, where he was the bakery manager. A handsome, kind and gentle man, he proposed four months later, at Lewes Rugby Club, the night England beat France in the (then) Five Nations. The year was 1990.

Irene rang me the moment she heard the news. Her first words to me were not "Hello", instead she asked, "Who is sitting on the Top Table, ducky?"

She was obviously very insecure about the wedding day. I decided to have a finger buffet to avoid any wedding politics. It had been 17 years since Mum, Dad, Irene and Eddie had seen each other. I was astonished to find out Mum wanted to sit with Dad in the church. I thought that was ridiculous! What a nightmare!

On 14th March 1992, Neil and I married. It was a wonderful day, albeit slightly fraught.

At the reception, Dad did not spend long on the father of the bride speech. He simply announced a toast, "To the bride and groom".

He did, however, speak to Mum for ages. I learnt afterwards this made Irene furious and caused a massive row, apparently.

I regret the decision I made to let Dad give me away, as he had no real part in my life. He had already given me away when I was five.

I should have asked my wonderful Uncle Ed to do it. What a consistent pillar of support he has been to me. I owe him so much. He hasn't featured in this story until now, so I will tell you unreservedly, he means the world to me. I doubt very much I would have survived without his support.

When I was 19, he invited me to stay with him in Indonesia where he was working. He worked abroad for most of his career, and this life-affirming trip truly lifted me at a low point. I was struggling with depression, but didn't know that then. I just felt shit. In the early years, before email, we regularly exchanged letters on the flimsy, blue Airmail stationery you had to use back then. I saved all his letters. I read them over and over, and they articulately portrayed his many adventures. His fabulous sense of humour was sprinkled across every page. One of life's great wits and a genuinely lovely person, he has had my back on many occasions. He is a total legend. (Thanks Ed x x x x)

A classic Ed moment is captured in the wedding video. Because we paid for our own wedding, and money was tight, the food budget was tight. The finger buffet was spread thinly over the table. Every single morsel of food was hoovered up as if a swarm of locusts had descended. The only items remaining were a complete pineapple (which had not been cut up) and a sad-looking half-eaten sandwich. A voice on the video can be heard announcing, "Neil and Rachel will now cut the cake!"

To which Ed responds, "Watch out! There'll be a stampede!"

I fell pregnant a year after our wedding, but we suffered a miscarriage 12 weeks into the pregnancy. We were both upset, but philosophical.

I worried about how thin Neil was getting. He was experiencing regular bouts of poor health. Despite this, we made a loving home together while he underwent several tests.

I fell pregnant again four months later. I was anxious and I cried when I saw the midwife. She thought I was worried about having another miscarriage, but it wasn't that. I opened up to her, telling her that I was afraid I wasn't good enough to be a parent. Through floods of tears, I told her I didn't think my children would love me, because my dad didn't want to be in my life and my mum had moved away to France. I had never realised how little I thought of myself until that point. I had always been a confident adult. I never knew I rated myself with zero self-worth.

She urgently arranged counselling. Something for which I will always be grateful.

I told my boss that I would be having a baby and wanted to take a step back whilst pregnant. I had made up my mind that I would do everything to look after myself. At 12 weeks, I had some small spotting, but was reassured at the hospital that all was well. I had a few more scans to keep an eye on things, but the pregnancy went well, and Neil and I totally loved our little baby already.

Neil and I discussed how we would manage raising our family. I wanted to be a stay-at-home mum. That was paramount. I'd happily go to work while the children were asleep, but I wasn't going to miss a moment.

I vowed at that moment that I would never let my children feel they were not worth spending time with. They would always be loved, and I would always make time for them.

This stayed with me throughout the challenging times ahead, as I continued working on my low self-worth and going to therapy.

My passion for continuous learning and personal development had blossomed.

On 22nd February 1994 we were over the moon when our beautiful baby, Joseph, was safely delivered by caesarean section. He was perfect and we instantly loved him so very much.

We had a lovely home, but it was a tough time financially. We had no central heating, which was hard with a small baby to care for. We had a log fire in the front room and a coal fire in the bedroom for warmth, but ice formed on the inside of the windows that winter.

Neil's health deteriorated. He had more tests to find out why he had lost three stone in weight and he suffered greatly with stomach problems. He looked poorly, but we were very loved-up.

To help with the finances, when Joe was nine weeks old, I took a part-time job back at Safeway, stacking the shelves at night, 8.30pm to 1am. I was still breastfeeding, which was problematic at times. It was no fun working with leaky boobs!

At this time, we heard the sad news that Neil's mum's cancer had returned, and she didn't have very long to live, but at least she got to meet Joseph. She died slowly over the next two years, after a long, painful demise. We were devastated.

Neil was only 13 when his dad had died, aged only 40. His mum only made it to 54. The week Neil's mum died, he was made redundant from Safeway – the only company he had worked for since leaving college. He fell into a deep depression, understandably.

I rang Mum and asked if she could come over for the funeral. I needed her to help me support Neil.

"But I didn't know the woman!" came the reply. It was true, she didn't. But that wasn't the point.

I didn't know how to tell her how she sounded. I had too much on my plate at the time. I didn't have the energy either, and I just got angry.

Neil found it too overwhelming to apply for any jobs. We survived on his redundancy pay and my small wage. Neil's brother, Keith (a senior nurse at the local hospital), urged him to try for a job in the casting department and pulled strings, so that Neil didn't have to have an interview. He was taken on as a casual Health Care Assistant to start with. Further down the line he developed a successful career as a Senior Orthopaedic Technician.

Money was extremely tight.

Despite the mini-pill and still breastfeeding Joe, I fell pregnant again. Our second baby came into the world on 14th December 1995. It was a traumatic experience, a crash caesarean, which meant the baby's heart beat was failing rapidly and they had to act fast. Not expecting to have surgery any time soon, I had only just eaten my lunch. They rapidly tried a spinal block to avoid anaesthetic. As they made their incision, I felt them cut me open. The block had failed. I screamed out. I heard them shout, "Get the dad out!"

A gas mask came rushing at me as two of the team pushed heavily on my chest.

Luke was delivered with no pulse, not breathing. He had an Apgar score of zero. Technically dead. The resuscitation team worked on him for a brief time.

Thankfully, I was unaware of that. When I woke a while later, I saw our beautiful, healthy baby, Luke, being cradled by Neil. We never knew why his heart had stopped. Luckily, I was at the hospital that particular day for a general check-up. I am eternally grateful to the midwife who checked me that day and the team that saved his life.

We were truly blessed to have him.

Joe greeted his newborn brother with so much love in his eyes. We were overjoyed. I cherish the photo that captures this moment. Our hearts soared. The boys were immediately best buddies. I loved that. It reminded me of how much my brother meant to me.

However, it wasn't all going to plan. Luke developed a problem when feeding and regularly choked at my breast. He would breathe in, but not breathe out. Then he would projectile vomit so violently that his sick shot off the end of our bed when I was sitting at the pillow end. It was horrendous. In between these bouts of choking and vomiting he was fine. I told the midwife, and she came and sat with me for two hours. She sat there patiently while I fed him. Nothing happened. I thought, "She thinks I'm mad." Two minutes after she left the house, Luke did it again. I cried whilst running up the road with Luke in my arms trying to wave her down in her car, but she didn't see me.

This went on for six weeks. I was crazy with worry every time it happened. Then the day for his six-week check-up at the clinic arrived, on that Friday afternoon. My sister-in-law, Sue (a nurse, Keith's wife), came to sit with Joe whilst I took Luke to his appointment.

Luke fed all the time. He had put on some weight, so seemed to be doing well. When the doctor laid him down to measure him, he listened to his chest and heard a crackle. When he mentioned it, I cried out "Thank God!" The doctor looked at me as if I was a mad woman.

I frantically told him what had been happening. I babbled and spewed out all the details of Luke's face turning purple, him not breathing out, the projectile vomit and how scared I was that he would die in my arms.

He made a call to book Luke in to see a paediatrician the following Monday morning at the hospital. I felt a wave of relief. It had not been helpful watching the news at that time. There were stories about cot deaths. Poor Anne Diamond. What a warrior she was to raise awareness whilst going through her own terribly sad loss.

I got back from the appointment and excitedly told Sue the developments. I was very relieved. I asked her whether she could look after Joe for me Monday morning whilst I took Luke to his appointment. She kindly said yes, and I fed Luke while she made us a cup of tea.

Right at that moment, Luke began to choke. She came in to see his little face all screwed up and purple. For what seemed like forever, he *would not* breathe in. She grabbed him and started to try to intervene, using all her years of nursing training. Then a jet of vomit shot across the room. He inhaled, gasping for breath, crying his little heart out.

Sue was beside herself with shock.

"Oh my God! Is this what you've been dealing with?" she gasped.

"You saw it! You saw it!" I replied, joining in with Luke, having a cry of relief.

It was the first time anyone other than Neil or I had seen what I had been trying to tell everyone about for six weeks.

She got straight on the phone to the doctor at the clinic. Luckily, she knew this particular doctor very well, because they studied at the same time and shared the same block of student accommodation.

"She can't spend all weekend like this with Luke in this state. He needs to be seen straight away!" she urged him firmly, but calmly. He listened and followed her guidance.

That night Luke and I went into hospital. I had to leave Joe, which broke my heart. This tender stage of bringing a new baby home can be unsettling, but I needn't have worried, Joe took it all in his stride.

The next few days were a roller coaster of emotions. At that time there was a wave of chest infections affecting babies and young children called Bronchiolitis (nowadays, this is mostly known as RSV). The admissions team took a swab from Luke and sure enough he tested positive. We had to stay in isolation from then on. It was a kind of see-through, plastic, tent-like structure with an air extraction system.

I didn't dwell on the recent news stories I'd seen on TV saying that 1 out of 10 babies with this infection become so seriously ill that they could die from complications.

They X-rayed Luke's lungs and came to tell me they had seen something of a shadow, which might be a mass or a possibly a hole. At this point I could no longer function sensibly, or take anything in. I began to rock backwards and forwards in my chair. "Can I phone my mum?" was all I could muster. I kept thinking about the Apgar score of zero.

They wheeled in the payphone trolley. I loaded it up with coins and dialled Mum, in France. The conversation didn't go well.

"I haven't got long, I'm on a payphone. I'm in hospital with Luke. He's choking. Can you come?" I had to shout, as Mum was going deaf. I didn't have much change, so there was no time for small talk.

"Oh, Rachel. Why do you always do this to me? I'm just going to Benidorm! I will call you when I get there," came the reply.

"When will I ever be allowed to need you?" I yelled. "Why can't you just come? Why can't you put me first? What's wrong with you?" I just kept shouting. "You didn't come when I had a miscarriage. You didn't come when Neil's mum died. I need you." The pips beeped and it was over.

I was frozen at the phone trolley in a stupor. I wished Mum could be a different person. I wished Dad could too. What was wrong with me that made it so hard for them to be how I wanted them to be? *I would never make my children feel like this!*

What I didn't know was that Mum meant to say that it would be quicker to get home from Benidorm than it would be from where she lived in France. In my head, *she just didn't want to spend time with me.*

A kind nurse came to disinfect the phone. She steered me back to my chair and fetched a cup of tea.

I couldn't tell Neil about that phone call. I tried to protect him from any stress for fear of making him unwell. He had recently been through hell with his bowel and had been diagnosed with Crohn's disease.

I fed Luke. He choked. The paediatrician came in at that moment and Luke's projectile vomit covered her from head to toe.

"Well, I think I now know what's causing all the trouble," she said.

She changed her apron, smiled and stretched out her arms to take Luke from me. "Come here, bonnie lad! You're a big fella for a poorly boy!" she crooned.

It was like an angel had come to help me. She was so wonderful, so kind, so caring, so professional and so informative. She provided hope.

She explained that having seen this episode, she knew what the problem could be. She said he might have underdeveloped, or weak, muscles in his oesophagus, which was causing the milk to collect and prevent his airways from working properly. My milk flowed so fast that breastfeeding wasn't helping.

She set out the course of action for the next few days. He would have to take some medicine to help push the milk down his oesophagus. The medicine would be mixed in with my breast milk and he would be bottle fed. We would monitor how it went from there. We would also set his cot mattress up at an incline to prevent any reflux. He was going to be given antibiotics for his chest infection. I asked about the shadow/hole on the X-ray and she said they would do another one in the morning.

The second X-ray was clear. Panic over! We followed the regime and Luke made great progress. Meanwhile, I asked a nurse if she would look at my caesarean scar, as it was stinging. She promptly told me to take a bath and she would be in shortly. I was puzzled, but followed her advice. I headed for the bathroom.

A few minutes later she came in with another nurse to look after Luke. I handed Luke over and got in the bath as directed. The nurse lanced a small boil at the edge of my scar, which gave the opportunity for a long string of puss to spue out into the bath water.

"Put this bag of salt in now and stay in resting for 10 minutes" she said firmly. "I'll come back shortly to check on you". Then she spun around and rushed off.

I hadn't noticed the deterioration in my scar. There was too much going on. It felt so much better.

The regime worked for Luke and the choking reduced. He recovered from the chest infection, and we were allowed home.

Mum rang me when she reached Benidorm, but I could hardly speak to her.

It was a bit strained for a while between us.

CHAPTER ELEVEN
TAKING THE BOYS TO SEE DAD

The boys were brilliant together. They were inseparable, until Joe started attending a fantastic playgroup. When Luke was nearly one, he decided he didn't like dropping Joe off and coming home without him. He wasn't going to miss out! He took things into his own hands. The drop-off became an unmanageable nightmare. He learnt how to unclip the buggy straps and ran off into the session like he owned the place. He caused such an uproar that the playgroup staff suggested that both of us stay. I needed to stay with him, so I became the playgroup treasurer/helper.

Apart from the fact that Joe woke like clockwork almost every hour, on the hour, every night and Luke never slept past 4.50am precisely (we never knew why that was), things were wonderful. Neil and I took turns to get up and play with the boys each morning, even though we were like zombies through sleep deprivation. We loved it, despite the toll it took on our beauty sleep.

Those boys were loved.

By 1996, I felt that I wanted to give my relationship with Dad another try. I hoped he might want to love my children like he did his other grandson. Dawn had a baby, Aaron, when she was 19. Dad thought he was great, and Ian told me how Dad raved about him.

I wanted Dad to love my boys. Another feeling hung over me all the time. *If I felt this much love for my boys, why didn't he feel like that about me?*

I bravely rang Dad to ask if we could visit him.

I wanted Ian to see my boys, too, and for us to meet Ian's son, Matthew, who was a little older than Joe.

I was chuffed to bits when Dad said yes AND *he sent me the train fare!* I was excited, he was never one for sending or spending money. *"This could be the beginning of something,"* I thought.

Travelling by train with Joe, aged two, and Luke, eight months, was hard work. I missed the connection at King's Cross as I struggled to cross London on the underground with the buggy, potty, bag and boys. I rang to let them know I had missed my train. Irene was horrid on the phone, "How *did* you manage *that*, ducky?" There was so much hostility in her voice. I recognised it instantly. I struggled to deal with my reaction at the way she spoke to me. It brought back all the reasons why I had stopped going to visit years before. With horror, I realised the weekend was going to be more difficult than I'd expected. The money for the fare hadn't changed anything else. I couldn't stop myself from saying something. I tried to be nice.

"Irene, I hope we will be able to get on OK this weekend. It's going to be difficult if we can't get on together." She immediately hung up. Oh God.

Dad collected me from the train station. He didn't greet me at all, silently putting the buggy and the bag in the boot, while I got into the back with the boys. He drove to the house without saying a word, while the boys chatted and babbled. I didn't try to engage him. It was obvious he was angry.

As we drove onto the driveway he turned off the engine, looked towards me and said, "Unfortunately, because you have upset my wife, you won't be able to stay here tonight. I can make you a cup of tea, but then you will need to find somewhere to stay."

As we went into the house, I was so enraged that a red mist descended across me, and I let rip with a barrage of pent-up anger and outrage. The exact words are a blur. He remained silent. He avoided looking at me. The boys played with the few toys I'd brought for them. I drank my tea. I booked a bed and breakfast for the night. We got back in the car. He dropped us off. I couldn't bring myself to say goodbye.

Me and the boys spent the rest of the weekend with Ian and his family. Dad came over and spent hours moaning about his life. I couldn't listen. I took the boys upstairs to play whilst he talked to Ian for the rest of the afternoon. When it came to the time he had to leave, he called me down and said, "Unfortunately I have had to choose between my wife and my children. Unfortunately for you, I chose my wife." I said, "OK, Dad." I leaned across and kissed his cheek. He left.

Later on, I did make attempts to offer olive branches, which had no effect. I decided to cut Irene out of my life. I sent a Christmas card just to Dad. He sent one back from "Rex and Irene", he had underlined Irene's name.

He sent one the following year signed "Rex (Dad)". So I sent one to him from "Rachel (daughter), Neil (son-in-law), Joseph and Luke (grandchildren)".

The lowest point in the horrible card exchange phase was when one arrived to 'Luke and Thomas'. I'm not proud of the way I dealt with that. "Who the fuck is Thomas?" I yelled down the phone. "Is it too much for you to get my children's names right?"

Well, was it?

As I write this now, I can sort of see why he might not have wanted to spend time with me. Was I expecting too much of him?

My boys never got Christmas or birthday presents or cards after that, and I blamed myself.

CHAPTER TWELVE

NEIL NEARLY DIES, JOE GOES TO

HOSPITAL

Poor Neil was extremely unwell with Crohn's disease.

On 25th August 1996, Neil's surgeon saved his live in a six-hour long emergency operation to remove most of his intestine and fit a colostomy bag. At 4am, after coming out of surgery, the surgeon rang me.

I was awake, sitting on the sofa with my wonderful, lovely, patient, calm friend Ruth. She had come to be by my side. The surgeon said, "I honestly don't know how Neil was walking on this planet. If I had left it an hour later he wouldn't have made it." Poor love. It was a devastating shock for him.

Throughout those early days with the babies and Neil's illness, Ruth was such a trooper and I cannot thank her enough for all her love and support. She became known as 'Where Would I Be Without You.' Neil wasn't getting better, despite the surgery and the dedicated care of the team.

Every day, I thought he would surely improve a bit, but he was just the same every day when I went to visit, only more dispirited.

I wanted to be with Neil, but it wasn't easy with the boys. Of course he wanted to see them, and when I was with him, I worried about them. When I was home with them, I worried about Neil.

Neil reacted badly to the morphine, which was why he was still so unwell. It wasn't until his brother Keith came to visit him that the mystery was solved.

Keith spotted Neil's white feet poking out the end of the bed and felt his legs – they were stone cold. Keith knew Neil's respiratory system was shutting down and Neil was losing the circulation in the lower half of his body. He immediately pressed the emergency alarm buzzer to alert the resuscitation team.

At that precise moment, I walked on to the ward with the boys, both in the double buggy babbling excitedly about seeing Daddy.

The buzzer was bleeping, Keith was pulling the curtains round, and doctors and nurses were appearing from everywhere. Neil was crying, terrified that he was about to die. "Let me see my boys, Rach! Bring them to me!" he called out.

A senior nurse ushered me and the buggy away to the waiting area and stayed with me until they had stabilised him. I tried not to alarm the boys, but I was shaking.

Once he was stable, I was allowed to take the boys in to see him. They loved their dad so much. He was tearful, but happy to see us. Poor Neil.

I got home and had to make a plan. I couldn't go on like this without help. I was worried about how we would all cope when Neil came home. There were a few things coming up which would add more pressure into the mix.

I braced myself and I phoned Mum to ask her to come home from

France to help.

"Can't Neil's sister help you?" she asked. "I'm right up to my eyes in sewage here. I've got a house full of guests to look after."

She worked for people with holiday homes managing the lettings. I had no idea what it was like for her at that time in her life. It was actually awful for her, but I didn't know and even if I did, I don't think I could have processed anything else anyway.

I'm not proud of it, but all I could do was shout at her down the phone. She rung off and the next day she fell ill having had a mini-stroke (TIA).

My nan rang to tell me off, telling me it was my fault. I shouted at her, too. Nobody knew what it was like for me. I was done with all of them. Why couldn't I just have one normal, caring parent?

I said to Nan, "At least she's got you to look after her. My husband nearly died, and nobody came to help me."

Not my proudest moment, but it was how I felt right at that point, despite the fact it was my lovely Nan at the other end of the line, who was trying to do the right thing for her daughter.

The morning after that dreadful phone call with Nan, Neil was due home.

I had to arrange carers for Neil, as he couldn't manage alone. I wouldn't be at home to look after him, because I had to take Joe to hospital to have his tonsils and adenoids out.

Joe had been unwell for a long time and the health visitor put in his little red book *"Failure to thrive"*. It cut like a knife. I wasn't going to postpone his operation. *He would thrive.*

At that exact time, Dad and Irene were in East Sussex visiting

Irene's father. They were just 10 miles away. I was stressed and needed someone to help. So, I rang him. He was my dad, after all…

Of course, he couldn't/wouldn't help. What was I thinking?

"Unfortunately, we won't be available to help you" he said. End of. I just put the phone down and moved on.

"No shit," I thought. I had really only called to ask him so that I could make sure *I still wasn't worth spending time with.*

My wide circle of wonderful friends stepped up and supported us. Fabulously supportive, funny and reliable Tina offered to look after Luke for the night, so I packed him an overnight bag and left him there – his first night away, ever. Luke loved Tina (I loved Tina!), but I still felt terrible leaving him there.

I packed up a handy bag of things for Neil, so that he had them at his side and made sure the nurse was coming as planned.

I packed up things Joe and I would need for the short stay in hospital and headed to the children's ward. Most importantly I remembered to pack Stinky Bunny, Joe's beloved, most favourite thing in the whole wide world.

Joe and I spent the rest of the day in the playroom. We had the place to ourselves. Bliss.

He had absolutely no idea about what was going to happen in the morning, and I didn't know how to prepare him. I was worried about Luke and worried about Neil and worried about Mum and worried that I had shouted at Nan. But my main focus was to love Joe, right there in that little bit of time we had, just the two of us.

Nobody tells you how hard it is when you have a second baby. You still love the first one as much as you did before, but you just have more things to do when the second one comes along. As if by magic more love flows out of you. It certainly flowed out of me.

I held Joe on my lap and tried to show him how much I loved him.

Joe eventually went off to sleep and I tried to sleep on the little camp bed next to where he lay.

Everything was rushing around my head. I was tired, but needed to be strong.

I'm not ashamed to say I prayed harder than ever before.

The morning came. I walked alongside Joe as the nurse wheeled him down to theatre.

The staff were fabulous with him. I held his little hand and kissed his beautiful little face while he drifted off. I didn't want to leave.

I was led out of the room by a kind nurse.

In the busy corridor, where people were bustling to and fro, she held me as I shook uncontrollably. No tears came. I was traumatised with stress. I felt numb.

When Joe woke up, he was angry with me for what had happened to him. He wouldn't look at me or let me hold him. I was mortified, but I did understand it from his perspective.

He took ages to settle and eventually I was able to stroke his soft mousy blonde hair until he drifted off. At that very moment, a ghost-like figure appeared at the foot of Joe's bed. It was poor Neil.

Of course he wanted to be with his son. I didn't blame him for that, but I couldn't cope seeing him looking so dreadfully woeful. I was empty. He still looked like death. His eyes were sunken, his skin was translucent, he was skin and bones, his clothes hanging off him. He woke Joe as he kissed him on the forehead. Joe began to cry and was then promptly sick. Bright red, blood-stained sick from the operation. Totally expected by the nurses, but horrific to us in our fragile states. I tried to soothe Joe, but he wanted Daddy. I walked out of the room in tears. I just wanted to be somewhere safe.

I wanted a different life. I wanted different parents. I wanted it to be better than this.

CHAPTER THIRTEEN
A VERY LOW POINT

Joe recovered very well and was much healthier and happier after his operation.

Neil, on the other hand, continued to have difficulties with hernias, Crohn's, infections and depression. Poor Neil. He hated that colostomy bag.

Money was extremely tight. I began to wonder how we would survive. It was touch and go whether we would be able to keep the house, but I couldn't let on to Neil. It got to the point where I found it difficult to buy food.

I called Mum to test the waters about whether I could ask her for a loan to see us through. Because I had got a frosty reception when I told her that I was pregnant with Luke ("Rachel! You can't afford to have another baby! How will you manage?"), I was very anxious about approaching her and admitting that we actually couldn't manage.

I approached her anyway, because I couldn't think of what else to do right at that moment.

Mum gave the request a cool reception, but thankfully she did offer a 'rescue package'. She posted 10 pre-signed, consecutively post-dated cheques for £50 so that I could cash one each week to buy food shopping. It was under the condition that I would pay her back and find a long-term solution to our situation.

"It's not right throwing good money after a bad situation," she commented.

She was right. We had to find a solution. *I* had to find a solution. Poor Neil was in no fit state to resolve anything.

And then a solution presented itself.

I was at the bank with my friend Mandy, cashing the first 'rescue cheque', when a group of students came in to cash their travellers' cheques. They were all wearing bright yellow sweatshirts with the words 'Jurgen Matthes Student Organisation' across the back.

"Foreign students… mmm that's interesting," I said out loud.

Mandy said, "I've heard it pays well."

Bingo! There was a solution staring me right in the face.

We began hosting foreign students in our dining room and spare room. The boys always shared a room anyway, so we effectively had two spare rooms for students. We made the most of the space we had to good effect.

We enjoyed it most of the time. The boys found it fun, too.

It was a bit hit and miss, though. Some students were delightful and we had a great time with them. Some were not so much fun, but the money was such a boost.

One rather grim situation scars me still.

We had three students with us who all caught a sickness and diarrhoea bug. Then the boys got it. Then Neil got it. Everyone, except me, was being sick and had the runs. We had one bathroom.

I strategically positioned buckets in various places.

My boys weren't having a great night, so I slept in with them. As I tried to drift off, I heard a knocking sound from the bathroom wall, which was on the adjoining wall to the boys' room.

I went to investigate. I knocked on the door. "Are you OK?" I asked, gingerly, thinking it might be one of our foreign guests.

"It's me, Rach. Come in," Neil whispered. He didn't want the students in the room the other side to hear.

I gently opened the door. The stench of diarrhoea overwhelmed me. Neil, and most of the bathroom, was covered in it. He was sobbing.

"I'm sorry, love," he cried. My heart went out to him. Poor, poor Neil. His bag had exploded. He was completely distraught.

"Don't worry, love. It's OK. Come on, I'll help you have a shower and get sorted," I replied.

I was straight into rescue mode. He had been through so much.

We took off the bag and I helped him get into the shower. He sobbed while I washed him all over. I got him a towel and ushered him into bed once we had replaced his bag.

After bleaching the whole bathroom down, having a shower and washing my hands a million times, I crawled into the boys' room again.

As I drifted off, exhausted from it all, but mainly exhausted from feeling sorry for Neil (and admiration for how he kept on every day, dealing with everything he was feeling), I heard a loud shriek from our bedroom. I hurried into the bedroom to find Neil hopping around the room.

"What is it, love?" I dared to ask.

"A fucking wasp has stung my foot," came the reply. "It was under the duvet."

"Are you jinxed? You couldn't make this up!" I said. We actually both started laughing and crying. I held him really close that night. Poor sod. I was glad his mum didn't have to see him go through this.

CHAPTER FOURTEEN
I'M DOING A DEGREE

Six months after the colostomy bag went on, Neil was allowed to have an operation to remove the colostomy bag. Thank God – so, back to hospital he went.

My dear friend from school, Sarah (my 'flatmate' of old), came to help. She knew how low I was, despite me trying to put on a brave face. We went together to see Neil after his op.

He was in a sorry state. It was quite a big deal, and he had been through so much, again.

When we left, Sarah asked me how we were coping, financially.

"We're OK. The student money helps," I replied, "But I'm not going to lie, we could lose the house if we aren't careful." It was a real and persistent threat, from which I tried to protect Neil.

"Rach, why are you waiting for this poor man to provide for you all? You've got qualifications and experience. You could go back to work," she offered.

And then it hit me. I did have a solution. I could provide. I would find a way.

I would have to give up this unrealistic and unhelpful dream that everything will be OK, and we can live 'happily ever after' and I can *be a perfect mum.*

"I want to be there for my kids. I don't want them to think I don't want to spend time with them…" I whimpered back. I sounded pathetic.

"Come on. Be real about it, Rach. This is shit and you know it." She was never one to mince her words. And she was right. I had to step up.

"Yep. It is."

So that was it. My stay-at-home mum dream was no more. I would start the very next day to make a plan.

And I did.

I researched for careers advice locally. I found an advisor operating in Brighton. I arranged childcare and got on the bus. On the journey I had a little cry. I knew it was the beginning of something challenging. I knew I would have to have someone other than me to look after my boys. *But I wanted them to know that they were worth spending time with.*

I deliberately set my mind to the future as I stepped off the bus.

I then had ninety minutes with a wonderfully helpful, wise and supportive, independent careers counsellor, who assessed everything about me, my qualifications and experience. She changed my life forever. (I wish I could remember her name. Thank you lovely lady, whoever you are.)

She spotted my BTEC Higher National Certificate in Business Studies (Merit grade) that I had achieved whilst working at GEC Avionics. Thank goodness I did that day-release college course!

She advised me that I could apply to university to become a Business Studies teacher with Qualified Teacher Status. The two-year course was a PGCE (Post Graduate Certificate in Education, a teaching qualification) plus a year conversion course to top up my HNC to a degree.

I thought this would be perfect. It meant that I would have a career where I could have the school summer holidays off with my boys!

Fancy that! It was the best £35 I could have spent.

Neil and I discussed it. At this point in time, he was not in a very upbeat state of mind. You couldn't blame him, after all he had endured.

He said, "As long as you remember that you have a family and we must come first."

I didn't want to think about the implications of studying for a degree at my age, plus looking after poor Neil, and running a home with two beautiful baby boys, then having a demanding career as well as my family. At least we would have the summer and Christmas holidays. I was through with retail at Christmas by this time!

I immediately set out making stuff happen.

I applied to university, researched funding for women retraining to return to the workforce and secured a grant from a charity to help cover the cost of a computer. I attended my university interview, got my place on the course and a grant from the Student Welfare Fund to help with some of the childcare costs.

I was all set to start the following September. Job done.

I felt so proud of myself and wanted to tell Dad that I was following in his footsteps. He qualified as a teacher later in life, too. (By this time, I had reached the ripe old age of 30.) It was some common ground between us.

I rang to tell him. But Irene answered.

"*You* won't be able to do *that, ducky!*" she said in her most hostile voice.

I would prove her wrong.

Mum was so pleased and proud. She never wanted to be a stay-at-home mum herself, and couldn't see any of the appeal of it. She was delighted that I would become a 'career woman'. She was never really that excited about me having children. Her experience of looking after children had traumatised her throughout her life. From the age of 13 she had to take responsibility for her three siblings. She didn't have a very happy childhood at all. Then the whole stepchildren thing hadn't gone well, either. She had lived a very hard life.

My biggest challenge was to work out how we could afford the rest of the childcare costs. Joe was three and a half. Luke was 18 months old.

I did manage it, though. By sheer luck, I found out about a scheme at our local college, which was looking for families with children, so that they could offer placements to childcare students. We were successful with our application.

The most wonderful female student called Naomi came to us. She was 19, totally fantastic, and it worked like a dream. (We were totally blessed to find you, Naomi. Thank you.)

After Naomi, came Nicky – similarly fabulous – then angelic Janice (Naomi's mum), then incredible Sheila. All of these beautiful people came into our lives and enhanced it with their love. We were so blessed with the caring, gentle, dedicated and reliable 'look-after ladies' during these years before the boys didn't need that care. RIP Janice.

The next challenge was to work out how I could fit in having a hysterectomy.

Bleeding constantly for a year after Luke was born had not helped me remain strong and robust. To cut that long story short, I couldn't go on for much longer getting run down and feeling weak.

It came to a head whilst I was pursuing options for childcare arrangements. I knocked on the front door of the home of a highly recommended childminder.

It was a particularly bad day for me. I was bleeding heavily, feeling dizzy and unwell, but I was on a mission to get everything sorted.

The lady opened the door to me, and I promptly fainted. I woke up on the floor whilst she was phoning the doctors across the road. She helped me over the road to the reception.

Within a few minutes, I was in with the doctor, who set about getting me on the list for a hysterectomy. I had a few tests in the following weeks and waited for the letter to arrive.

My enrolment day letter arrived for my Brighton University course. It was 28th October 1997.

My hospital letter arrived with my operation planned for 16th October 1997.

I needed another plan.

All the advice given ahead of the operation was about taking it easy and not lifting, blah, blah, blah. I immediately panicked about not being able to lift up my boys to sit them on my lap, or do all the mum things I loved doing with them. I considered abandoning the operation altogether.

I phoned Mum.

"You've got to have it done. It's the best thing I ever did. I will help you. I'll do anything other than look after the children. I will cook and clean and shop and all that, but don't leave me with the boys."

I totally understood her in that moment. *She could not cope with children or being a parent.*

"That's great, Mum. Thank you."

It wasn't what I wanted. But it was something. I was finally beginning to understand Mum.

What I actually wanted her to say was: *"I would be honoured to come and love those beautiful little babies of yours. I love them so much and miss them every day. I can't bear to live in France now they are in my life. I must come back to England and move near to you, so I can be in your lives and support you."*

But that is just not who she is.

Finally.

I realised.

She was traumatised and I had to love her for who she was. She couldn't be what she wasn't.

I had to give up expecting her to be what she couldn't be. I was beginning to understand 'acceptance'.

The resistance is the suffering.

And then I remembered something from years before.

I was 13 years old. It was the day I started my periods. I came home from school and told her. She said, "Did you feel sick?"

"No, Mum. I just had some pains in my tummy," I replied.

"I was sick with mine. You're lucky. I had dreadful periods all my life." She then went on to say something I didn't fully understand at the time, but it suddenly came back to me a few moments after the call I'd made about my looming hysterectomy.

"Well, you can get pregnant now. So, watch out! I'm telling you straight. If you ever come home to me and say you are having a baby, I will disappear from your life. You see these keys?" She waved the house keys in front of me.

"Yes," I replied, confused.

"If you get pregnant, I will throw the keys to the house to you and I will be gone. You won't see me for dust!" She glared at me, and I truly believed her.

I had totally forgotten that, until this latest phone call. Right there and then, I completely got it. There was her trauma staring me right in the face. I couldn't process it back then. She had frightened me and I had blocked it out. I couldn't understand then, but I got it right now.

She couldn't cope being a parent. She was afraid I might not cope either.

She did come home from France to help me, and she was excellent at all the things she *is* so good at. She didn't know how to be around the boys, though, she thought they were too demanding.

"They want you all the time," she kept saying. "When you were little, I didn't know I had you. You played in your bedroom." I wasn't sure that was true. I could read at the age of five. Who taught me that?

She did try her best, though, and I appreciated it.

Mum was fabulous the day I enrolled at uni. I couldn't stand for long, so she stood in the queues, holding my place, so that I could remain sitting as instructed by the doctor. She called me when the time came for me to sign a form or do anything else. She made sure the staff looked after me and told everyone how proud she was of me. It was great. In fact, she was a real source of strength and support while she came to stay.

She just wasn't really that interested in my lovely boys.

The two years at university were some of the best and worst days of my life. Suffice to say it was very demanding. I loved the learning and the people, but it was a big undertaking with the boys, Neil's ill health, the financial worries, the studying, and the school placements which meant I had lessons to prepare, schoolbooks to mark, uni work to complete and everything else running a home entailed.

By June 1999, I was the proud recipient of a degree with a 2:1 Hons Business Education, QTS.

Neil, Ian and Tina were in the crowd to cheer me on at my graduation ceremony. Dave and Ann Whitton were outside to greet me afterwards. Mum couldn't come over for that.

I felt good about myself. I was also feeling terrified that I had bitten off more than I could chew.

I sent Dad my graduation photo. He sent it back saying that it was 'inappropriate'. That was a low moment.

I need to mention a significant friendship from my uni days. Sam Alvarez and I were on the course together. We gelled instantly and have remained friends ever since. At end of the course she moved to the USA to marry Jonny. She came back to the UK when her baby, Mia, was due. Sam's mum looked after Mia and my boys for two years, as they progressed through school, for which I am extremely grateful. I am in total awe of Sam for all her wondrous strength and determination. She is a legend.

CHAPTER FIFTEEN
TEACHING BUSINESS STUDIES

I started my teaching career aged 32, on the 1ˢᵗ September 1999. I could start earning a decent wage. I was promoted the following year and Neil got a bit better, too.

Luckily I was able to take Joe to his first day at school. Unfortunately, I wasn't able to get the day off when it came to Luke's turn. I was distraught about that, but I'm not sure he was too bothered! Our lovely 'look-after lady', Sheila, was brilliant.

In 2001, I took another job closer to home at the local Sixth Form College. It paid a bit more money and gave me some more responsibilities. Almost every year after that, I took on a more senior role and increased my salary.

By 2009, I was a Senior Tutor, managing a big team of tutors, with several responsibilities across the college in addition to my classroom teaching duties. But more about 2009 later.

How wonderful it was for me that Sam Alvarez came to join me at the college in 2002.

Part of my role meant that I regularly delivered staff training, which I found very rewarding.

In 2003, I trained to mark the A-Level Business Studies exams.

Once I got used to it, I found I could mark a whole paper within 25 minutes. I was actually extremely slow, because I really loved doing it! I found it really helped my teaching practice. I knew exactly what students needed to do to reach the best grades. That was an added bonus, however, my main reason for doing it at first was to generate enough income to pay for us all to have family holiday abroad. I was fairly effective in that regard. We spent a week at an all-inclusive resort in Rhodes! It was brilliant. I marked over 1000 papers that year! What was not so great was having to get up at 5am to get a few more done before work, though! My respect goes out to all those teachers who mark school assessments. It is hard work. The exam system doesn't seem set up to cope properly with one of its main objectives, unless it relies on people who are prepared to sacrifice their free time to earn a little extra. Slightly demotivating knowing that at least 25% of what they earn goes straight back to the government!

Sam Alavarez asked me whether I would be willing to take the exam I was teaching as part of a research project she was undertaking. My high regard for Sam meant that I felt privileged to be asked and said yes straightaway. I was actually entered for the exam in the same way the students were – all officially – because Sam wanted to request my exam paper back to investigate the skills of evaluation and analysis.

I never really gave it much thought – I agreed on the grounds that it would be helpful.

The day came and a sudden realisation hit me: "What if I failed?!" It was too late then to back out, and I just had to suck it up. I completed all three papers and they were sent off with the rest of them. Obviously we couldn't mark our own papers!

On results day (a huge day for the college), the Principal called me into his office. I didn't know for what. I headed up the stairs full of data about my students and whether or not we had hit our targets. It was usually a day fraught with spreadsheets and analysis.

As I knocked and entered the Principal gestured for me to take a seat.

"Oh God!" I thought, "I failed the exam!"

"Rachel, I've had a letter from the Exam Board regarding your paper," he announced with a serious look on his face.

I went cold. I began preparing an apology in my head thinking that I had embarrassed the reputation of the college and made a fool of myself.

"There's one here for you, too," he went on. "Mine tells me that my student Rachel Stone has performed extremely well in the A-Level Business Studies exam, having achieved one of the top five highest marks in the country." He stopped speaking and passed my letter to me. "What about that, then?!" he said as a massive smile broke out across his face.

I was speechless. I hadn't even revised. I just didn't have time.

Thank goodness I had trained as an assessor!

I don't mind saying that it remains one of my proudest moments.

Anyway…

A turning point came in 2004, when the Sixth Form College merged with the FE College next door. Then began a learning journey, which led me to start my own leadership and management journey of personal development.

That summer, Mum invited us to spend a week's holiday with her in

France. Joe was ten and it made me think. Ian was ten when 'the swap' happened.

Mum and I sat having a cup of tea, while Neil had taken the boys for a walk along the river. I asked her, "How did you come to the decision to let Ian go with Dad and Irene. I could never let Joe go."

She completely collapsed, sobbing hysterically, and said, "There is not a day that goes by that I don't regret what happened when I think about how it turned out."

I had never seen Mum so distressed until then. I realised that she was carrying that around with her all the time.

She explained her reasoning, saying that she thought that Ian would be better with his real dad than with another man – especially coming up to being a teenager. She also thought that Eddie was too possessive and pushy to be able to cope with Ian and he might be jealous.

She did what she thought was best at the time. She hoped it would be good for him. The stupidity of what she did in the heat of the moment meant everything went terribly wrong. What started as a silly, fashionable attempt to spice up their sex lives – a partner swap – ended in a complete mess.

She has been on a journey and it is a fascinating story. She has written her story about the experience in a fiction book, based on real-life events, under the pen name Kay Moriarty. It is called The Husbands Next Door.

It was a tough read for me, but I learnt a lot about her.

I left teaching in 2012 to set up my own company as a business coach and a leadership and management trainer. The second part of this book is dedicated to sharing that journey and my learning and experiences with you.

Before we go there to Part Two, there's a few more significant parts of the puzzle.

CHAPTER SIXTEEN

A VIRUS

In November 2006, I was unwell with a flu bug. More than unwell, actually, I couldn't stand up. I spent the entire half-term holiday in bed, I didn't even get dressed for a week.

After the break, I returned to work, but could not get going.

One evening I popped into town for a few bits of shopping before M&S closed. I thought I would pop there for a ready meal, because I couldn't face cooking. It was nearly closing time, so I thought I would run there to be sure of making it.

I physically couldn't run. My body would not do as I urged it. I found that very strange, because I was very fit.

The next day at work I thought I was coming down with a chest infection, because my chest ached.

A week later I thought I ought to make an appointment after a colleague at work said, "Are you ok, Rach? You look like death!"

"Charming!" I thought.

I took a look in the mirror and she wasn't wrong. Perhaps I did have a chest infection. Funny I wasn't coughing, though.

I made an appointment and saw the doctor the next day. He listened to my chest and said, "Your heart rhythm is a bit out, let's do an ECG."

I sat a short while waiting for the ECG machine to become free. The results showed a slight irregularity.

"I'll arrange for some further tests," the doctor said.

I wasn't worried. I was just glad I didn't have a chest infection.

I was fit, I wasn't overweight. I didn't drink much, I had never even as much as held a cigarette and I'd only had flu.

To my surprise the appointment came through for the following Tuesday. Luckily, the timeslot fitted in right where I had a gap in my teaching timetable. Another bonus was that the college is situated right next door to the hospital.

I strode across the small field to the appointment as rapidly as I could to get there on time.

They carried out the test where you walk on a treadmill whilst wired up to the monitors. They increased the speed and the incline, and I had to get off. I thought I was going to die!

That sounds a bit overdramatic, but it was painful and scary.

I walked slowly back to work.

The next morning, I had a call from the consultant's secretary asking me to go to see the consultant the next day.

So, I did.

I was given a spray for angina and an appointment for an angiogram. I was also told to refrain from exerting myself.

"Blimey," I thought, "I must be getting old. I haven't got time for this, really."

After the angiogram I was highly relieved to be told there was nothing wrong and I could get on with my life.

Thank goodness for that.

It was a shame that the following couple of years were a little spoilt at times by periods of total fatigue, fainting episodes and general exhaustion, interspersed with feeling totally OK.

I thought it was all in my head, but I found standing up teaching all day and rushing around took its toll on me.

I had periods of feeling quite low, because I missed the person I used to be (i.e. the one who was extremely active and buzzed about all the time, not the one who had to lie down for two hours after shopping in Tesco.) It was still a mystery.

My genius GP had heard of a new thing called POTS (Postural Orthostatic Tachycardia Syndrome). He thought I could be experiencing the symptoms of this. The way to diagnose it was through a 'tilt test'.

I was sent for that, during which I was strapped to a bed which could be tilted, hence the name. Readings were taken of my pulse and blood pressure, whilst laying horizontally, then the bed was tilted vertically to compare the measurements in the new position.

I fainted immediately when the bed pivoted.

And there it was.

The signals to my heart weren't working correctly in conjunction with my spine. My pulse raced frantically instead of adjusting steadily, then it plummeted to a pathetically low rate.

It became apparent after that test that my resting heart rate had dropped significantly from a normal level to a very low 40 beats per minute by this time, in 2010. This had probably started when I was unwell in 2006, having had the virus initially.

Stupidly low blood pressure was also affecting me, so, in a nutshell, at times I wasn't getting enough oxygen in the important organs to function properly. In between that I was perfectly OK.

No wonder I was flagging from time to time. It was difficult to explain to people before I knew what was going on. They would say things like, "You were alright to go out yesterday, but you can't even climb the stairs today."

I truly believed that everyone (including Neil) was thinking that I was making it all up.

Obviously, I wasn't and it was such a relief to know that there was something I could work on to solve the problem.

Researching the condition was easy because of the internet, so I found loads of great tips on how to manage it, once I knew what it was I was dealing with.

The best thing I could do to help myself was to get extremely fit to improve something called 'venous return'. The thing that made me feel terribly ill was exercise, it rendered me useless afterwards for hours on end.

I took some advice about my work situation from my union rep.

"You should take a year off sick and worry about yourself. Get fit but lay down when you need to! Simple! You get quite a lot of time on full pay, so why don't you do that?"

In hindsight, it might have been a good idea.

However, I knew that if I went off sick, it was unlikely that anyone would be brought in to cover my work as a direct replacement, so most likely my colleagues (my fabulous team) would be picking up the slack.

I knew my own head. I doubted that I would be able to relax knowing that I had landed my team in the proverbial pile of dog-doo. I wasn't prepared to drop them in the shit.

Standing up all day was no longer something which brought the best out in me. I just couldn't handle it, so I decided I needed to make some lifestyle changes.

Whilst pondering my options that week, one of my students helped me come to a decision, which would see me move in the right direction.

A bubbly BTEC student said during the lesson, "You know a lot about businesses, Miss, but you haven't got one. Why's that?"

Mmm. Good point!

So, I decided to review my skills and see what I needed to learn in order to sort that out.

I undertook some professional development in the shape of a Small Business Coaching Diploma with The Coaching Academy. It fitted the spec for the plan I was formulating for my new life. I worked on this during my spare time in the evenings, weekends and holidays, which basically meant quite late at night and the odd trip for group tutorials on a few Saturdays over the course of the next 18 months.

I left full-time, permanent employed work in 2012. I'll tell you about how I set up my own business in Part Two. But there's something I need to share with you first.

CHAPTER SEVENTEEN
DAD HAS TWO YEARS TO LIVE

In April 2013, when Luke was 18, Dad phoned to tell me he had a maximum of two years to live. He was dying of prostate cancer. I was shocked and didn't know how to respond. I said I was sorry to hear about this. I asked him questions about his situation and listened carefully. I also asked if I could phone him to check on his progress from time to time. He said that it was best if I didn't.

Luke overheard me on the phone and asked me what the call was about, so I told him.

He immediately asked if he could see his Granddad Rex. Both his other grandparents had already died before he was born. He really wanted to meet this granddad.

I could not find a reason to say no to Luke. It was 17 years since the disastrous incident when I missed the train connection. My boys never saw Dad after that. I'm not sure I did, either.

Mum was visiting me from France at the time. She didn't like the idea of me driving all that way with only Luke in the car. So Mum, Luke and I drove to Lincoln. She also might be able to see Ian.

Joe wasn't interested.

We both expected her to have to wait in the car at Dad's house. I couldn't be sure we would be allowed in. At least we might be able to see Ian. No worries if not. At least I would have tried to fulfil Luke's request anyway.

I was painfully aware that we were making an unannounced visit, which was a brave move, *but I had been told not to phone*. What else could I do?

We knocked on the door of the house I thought to be Dad and Irene's address. I was rather nervous, as I stood there bearing gifts, my tall, slim son at my side and Mum sitting patiently in the car.

"They've moved. We bought this from them a few years ago," the friendly chap said.

I explained who we were and he obligingly gave us the forwarding address he had for the former owners.

So they'd moved, but not told me. Nice.

At this point, I rang Ian and said that I was in the area with Mum, and asked him if he and his family could meet us for dinner. Somewhat puzzled, he said yes. I knew instantly that he was tense about it. He knew that Irene would quiz him if she found out. Little did he know we were heading right to her new house at that precise moment!

As we stood on the doorstep of the address we had just been given (a smart bungalow on a fairly modern development with very tidy gardens), Irene popped her head out through a small crack in the doorway to prevent the yapping dog at her heels from escaping. She obviously didn't recognise me. "And you are?" she asked.

I said, "It's Rachel."

She tried again "Who are you?"

She seemed very old. I had not seen her since my wedding, nearly 23 years previously.

"It's Rex's daughter," I replied.

Her eyes widened with shock, and she said, "You'd better come in."

Luckily, my stepsister, Dawn, was inside. She was very chatty and friendly and was very interested to find out about Luke. Her own son, Aaron, was there too and we exchanged pleasant introductions. He looked very much like his mum.

Irene called Dad and said, "You'd better get dressed, your daughter's here."

Dad padded out in his pyjamas, looking dishevelled and understandably grey-skinned. I was shocked by his baldness from his chemo treatment. He had always had such smart, tidy, thick blonde hair. He looked first to Luke and unexpectedly said, "I'm sorry I haven't seen you before now."

Luke was quick to reassure him, as is his usual charming manner, "That's OK, Granddad."

Dad looked and me and said, "Hello". I leaned over and kissed his cheek.

Dad retreated to get dressed and Luke and I were offered a cup of tea. In the kitchen, Irene reached into a cupboard, took out a crystal glass and announced, "I'm not an alcoholic, ducky, but I am having a brandy."

I had no real appreciation of how much my unannounced visit would cause her so much anxiety.

I justified my actions to myself in a repeating inner monologue.

"Dad rang to tell me he hadn't got long to live. What did they expect?" was on repeat inside my head.

Perhaps he hadn't told her he had rung me…

As the minutes ticked by, things got easier. We all gathered in the living room, where I gave Dad and Irene their gifts. An orchid plant for Irene and a book all about interesting, historical buildings in Eastbourne for Dad.

Dad was pleased and chatted with Luke about lots of things, rambling a bit, switching to new topics rapidly. Luke kept up his interest, whilst Dawn and I chatted about the joys of being a mother of teenagers.

I kept thinking that I had no real grasp of what her life had been like and she knew nothing of mine, despite having lived as sisters for a good chunk of our lives and experiencing the trials and tribulations of the fall out of that fateful holiday in 1972. I recalled the time we really fought like wild cats in a ditch across the field opposite Dad's house that summer. I think that was the last time I had seen her.

Meanwhile, as we drank our tea and made small talk, the phone rang. It was Alison, my other stepsister. Irene asked if I'd like to her to pop over to join us. She could be with us within 20 minutes.

At this point I remembered Mum was in the car outside! We had not expected to be allowed in. I'd forgotten she was stuck out there, waiting.

"I'd love to see Alison, but Mum's outside in the car and I can't leave her too much longer, as she may need a comfort break."

Dad called out, "Go and get her in! You can't leave her out there. Bring her in!" he was ordering me.

I was shocked! They had not spoken since my wedding and that had

caused Dad and Irene to argue on the day, but I did as I was told. I had
no idea where this was all heading.

I popped out to the car and asked Mum to come in. She said she
was nervous, but as she needed the loo, it was a good idea.

"Hello Kay, d'you want a cup of coffee?" Irene crooned, as if they
had remained best friends over the last 40 years.

"Ooh, yes please, I'm gasping," Mum responded appropriately.
"Could I use your loo?"

And then I sat, transfixed, watching this bizarre scene unfold, where
everyone chatted and caught up on news, as if none of the misery of
before had ever existed.

Alison came in and gave me and Mum a really big hug. She was so
pleased to see us all and she engaged in friendly banter with Luke.
Photos of Dawn's and Alison's children were passed around. Irene
asked Mum what living in France was like.

I looked on in disbelief and didn't really speak much.

After a short while, Dad realised he needed to get ready to go out
for a blood test and we made our exit. We all hugged and kissed each
other goodbye and headed back to the car. Dad and Irene waved us off
and we drove out to the main road.

Luke was confused. "Mum, how come they can be so nice to me
and you *today*, but for all these years it's been so horrible?"

"It's complicated, Luke," I replied, "People do their best at the time
and is not always what you want."

It was all I could muster, because I was equally confused.

"Being diagnosed with a terminal illness does change people," I thought.

I was considering letting myself call the visit a success. It certainly had made Mum feel better to see Dawn and Alison and to receive such a warm welcome. She said it felt like closure.

When we arrived back in Eastbourne, I tried to process how weird it all had been. I ran through it over and over in my mind. I had actually said very little to Dad and he really only chatted with Luke, but it was difficult to follow that conversation.

At the end of the second day back at home, Dad rang.

He said in an agitated tone, "Don't call round uninvited again. That was a stupid thing to do. You've upset my 'good lady wife'."

I remained calm.

"Dad, you told me *not to phone you*, but you didn't say I couldn't visit."

I knew it would annoy him, because it was a subtle, but true, view of his instructions earlier that year.

I had been expecting something like this, if I am honest. I knew it would come, because of Irene's manic texting to Ian. A day earlier, Ian rang to say that Irene sent him three or four text messages as we left her, frantically demanding to know whether he had known beforehand.

She demanded to know if he had kept information from her. Classic Irene.

Of course he hadn't known, because I knew it would stress him out, so I didn't tell him. I also knew he could be in for some grief, because I had disturbed things. Nothing had changed there. I hoped he would get off lightly. I felt guilty, but Luke had made a reasonable request. After all, he just wanted to see his granddad before he died and why couldn't he?

"Dad, you rang me to tell me you are dying. What did you expect me to do?" I interjected into the silence. "Luke asked if he could meet you. I couldn't think of a reason why he would not be allowed. What would you want me to say? 'Granddad doesn't want to see you'?"

"You are so bloody-minded and stubborn," he offered.

I tried to explain that despite not being part of his life, we all still cared about him and were worried about him in his poorly condition. I tried to be kind – he was dying, after all.

It ended with a promise from me not to phone, *or visit*. I wished him well with his treatment. I sent them a thank you card and left it at that.

Dad spent his entire life and his limited wealth on pandering to Irene and her girls, then subsequently to the girls' children. This had to be. It was saving his second marriage. It was at the expense of his relationship with his own children and his other family members. Only one of Dad's three sisters was *allowed* to be in contact with him. The other two upset his 'good lady wife', apparently. There was a lot of that about.

A year later, Dad phoned to tell me he had *found religion*. His call was to tell me he had *forgiven me*. I didn't take too kindly to that.

He was clumsy, really. I put it down to the illness or the medication. He also said, "I had a lovely 80th birthday meal. All my family was there."

I was astounded that he actually said that.

"Not all your family, Dad. I wasn't there, and neither were my boys. We are your family too."

I tried really hard to say it kindly.

He said, "Oh yeah. I have to be careful what I say to you, don't I?"

It was a difficult phone call, because I so desperately wanted to make him feel better about everything. I wanted to rescue him and to '*be good*'.

I struggled to accept that he wasn't curious about my children, or that he didn't feel the powerful love for me that I experienced for my children. I felt he didn't love them.

It was hard for me to think that he didn't consider me and my boys his family. I really wanted that comment to be just a stupid/drug-induced mistake.

I ended the call by saying that I loved him and would help him if he needed anything as his condition worsened. He thanked me.

He phoned again a few weeks later. I felt like he was calling to ask me to forgive him, so I gushed loads of reassuring phrases, but deep inside I just wished I could hear him say he was sorry, out loud, and that he'd like to be close to me before he dies.

It is funny (peculiar) that when his 'friend request' came through on Facebook, I was thrilled. I sent a little message: "Hi Dad, how are you doing. I hope you are OK." He sent back, "Hi Rachel and family. I am fine and Irene is fine. I hope you are all OK."

I wasn't interested in how Irene was, actually. *I am sure that if it were possible he would have underlined the Irene part.*

I found myself wondering how he was a lot of the time. *How much time did he have left? Was he OK? What was he thinking? Was he in pain?*

On my way home one day I stopped in a layby. I just needed to know. I was compelled to call. Irene answered. "I'll get your Dad, darling." That shocked me. She was tender, not hostile.

Dad and I chatted a little bit, but he was stilted and curtailed the conversation.

I said, "I was just thinking about you and hoped you were OK". He said he was, so we rung off.

I didn't call again. I wasn't allowed. That was clear, if not a bit confusing.

Dad died in 2016.

He deteriorated relatively quickly. Ian called me. He said that Dad might only live another three days.

It was the day Neil and I moved into our new house, and I was unloading the removal lorry. The move was an attempt to rebuild our marriage. Things weren't going too well. Neil was suffering terribly with a trapped nerve in his neck (poor sod), so he couldn't do much. In fact, he could barely move, so he could hardly drive me to Lincoln. He wasn't a fan of Dad, either. You couldn't blame him. I had done nothing but cry about him since we met!

Even if Neil was fit, he wouldn't want to visit, but he would have taken me. Of course.

As luck would have it, Mum was staying with us, to help us move. What a trooper.

She had recently moved back from France to live in Thanet. Nan had came back to England as Granddad had died and Mum came back soon after that.

Mum was always very practical. Like a little ball of energy and *so* organised. She was brilliant supporting me with the move. Always able to crack great jokes, too.

I wanted to go to Dad. She didn't want me to go alone, so we set off together. I called Ian to let him know.

I knew it might be difficult for Ian if I visited, as it always upset

Irene, however, she was very pleasant on the phone when I called to ask if I could see Dad.

My feelings were mixed. I knew deep inside I was going there because I needed to hear Dad say something to reassure me, something along the lines of, "I have always loved you. I'm so proud of you. You are a lovely girl." Any, or all, of those…

I wanted that so much. I was afraid I wouldn't hear it, but very keen to have that chance.

I dropped Mum off at Ian's. I went to Dad and Irene's. I was very shocked at his condition. Irene did her best to prepare me.

Credit where credit was due, she was kind, despite how she must have been feeling.

She was stoic.

Dad's sister Anne and her husband were staying at the house. Anne is the one sister who Dad still had a relationship with. She came to help. It was more than 30 years since I had seen Aunt Anne. She hadn't changed much, but she did have a new husband. This husband Pete wasn't my *original* Uncle Peter. She had re-married, and her new husband had the same name. That's handy, I suppose!

He was very nice to me and completely aware of the difficulty of the unfolding situation.

Anne and Irene tended to Dad before I was allowed in to see him. In the few quiet moments that Pete and I sat quietly together in the kitchen, he said, unexpectedly, "This must be very hard for you."

"What makes you say that?" I asked.

"You don't exist," he replied, looking around the room at all the photos of Dawn and Alison and their children. One wall was completely filled with photos in frames, capturing all manner of occasions and celebrations, but not one of us. Loads of family photos but not one of Ian, his children or me and my family. Not even my wedding photo was seen amongst the others.

"I know," I replied "I have sent photos. I sent my graduation photo in 1999. It came back with a note which said it was inappropriate to have sent it."

He raised his eyebrows and then gave a me look which said, "I get it".

The feelings that flooded over me seeing Dad in this pitiful state were totally unexpected. I felt so much for him. They washed over me like a wave. I hugged him and stroked his hair. I kissed him and held his hand. How weird? Nothing between us for years and then my feelings swamped me. He was not able to do or say much. He asked me to leave after a few minutes.

I thought he would die that night. I did not know how to feel.

I stayed up late with Mum and Ian. Irene rang the next day to say Dad was in hospital and much better. They had drained lots of poison from his infected knee and he was responding well to treatment.

I decided to call into the hospital on my way home to say goodbye. Ian met me there. Mum came in for a cup of tea and a loo stop before we set off. She waited in the corridor.

Both Ian and I sat next to Dad's bed and chatted a bit. He seemed able to talk a bit more, but wasn't fully himself. I wondered whether he'd like to see Mum, so asked him gingerly, "Mum's in the corridor, would you like to say hello?" (I thought, actually, he might like to say goodbye.)

"Go and get her! Hurry up!" he said with as much authority as he could muster.

I called her in. She approached him carefully. "Hello, Tinker," he said.

The softness and his smile really shocked me. She sat next to him and immediately held his hand. He didn't mind at all.

"*What would Irene make of this?*" I wondered.

They chatted for a few minutes. Then Dad got nervous and agitated as he looked at the time. He told us we ought to leave, before Irene came.

It was odd, there together as a family, just us four. It had been 44 years.

As we left, I blew him a kiss. He wasn't looking. I didn't think I would see him again.

Mum felt good that she had had a chance to say goodbye.

For a few weeks more he struggled on. Now and then I rang the ward to see how he was.

Then, one day a nurse from the ward called me.

"Is that Rachel? Mr Tanner's daughter?" she asked.

"Yes, that's right." I replied.

"He asked for you today. He wondered where you were."

As soon as I heard this, I shot straight up there. Neil drove me – we set off within a few minutes of me putting the phone down. (Thanks, Neil.)

I took a photo with me which was from the summer holiday which

Neil, my boys and I had been on that July. I wanted to put it by his bedside.

We arrived four and a half hours later. Neil waited in the car.

Dad wasn't really with it, he was rather confused.

I so desperately wanted to hear something loving. Once more, I fussed over him and held his hand, telling him I loved him.

In desperation, I said, "You *do* love us, don't you, Dad?" showing him the photo, feeling so needy as the words fell out of my mouth.

He tried to smile, then looked away. He shut his eyes to drift off to sleep. I stayed a few more minutes and said my last goodbye.

I thanked the nurse for contacting me. I got back in the car with Neil, who had stayed in the car park. He drove me home.

That was the last time I saw Dad.

CHAPTER EIGHTEEN

AWAKENING, MY TRANSFORMATION

In the silent journey home, I realised so much. It was a transformation of awareness shifting in me. Finally.

Dad was just being himself. He was who he was, and I hardly knew him, really. Why did I expect so much of this man?

He was just trying to do his best with his level of capability.

We all do our best.

None of us are perfect.

The many years I'd spent (and the considerably large investment I'd made) on personal development, training and learning to become a manager in my employed work, and a business coach in my self-employed work, had paved the way for me to transform myself.

I had simply forgotten to apply this learning to myself.

How many times had the power of gratitude come up in coaching sessions about mindset as part of sessions with business clients?

Most likely hundreds of times.

(Take my advice – I'm not using it!)

In that car, in the dark, on the motorway, the Tarmac whizzing beneath the tyres, putting the physical distance between the old me and the new, *more adult* me, sitting silently next to my husband, my marriage in a state and my dad on his death bed, I made a massive shift.

What has all this taught you? Where is the learning from your experience?

You can dwell on gratitude if you choose to.

Answers came flooding in.

You don't need external validation.

You don't need Dad's approval.

You are your own person, and you are strong.

You are OK.

You are safe.

The person asking to spend time with you, is yourself.

Suffering comes from resistance.

You must learn to accept that *only you can only find your own self-worth.*

Nobody can give you that now. You are an adult.

You have to find it within you.

So, I came to dwell on gratitude.

The day of Dad's funeral arrived. Neil and the boys did not want to come, but Mum wanted to be in the car with me on the journey to Lincoln and back. That way she could spend time with Ian and his family. Irene had stated that she didn't want Mum to attend, which was upsetting for Mum, because she would have liked to have seen Dad's sisters and to be there in the crowd. She fell into line because nobody wanted a scene. She waited back at Ian's house. I had one small request regarding the funeral. I asked Dawn to ensure that the photo of my family was placed in with Dad in the coffin. She said she would make sure this was done. (Thank goodness for Facebook Messenger.)

I knew I wanted to say something on the day. *I wanted to be able to thank him.*

Everyone gathered in the church for the religious service, which was pleasantly done.

Irene looked fragile, but dignified. Her girls were very caring and her grandchildren stayed right by her side throughout.

I was greeted warmly by them all. I'd bought Irene a little gift, a bottle of Bach's Flower Remedy to drip under her tongue. I'd heard that it was good for soothing distress. She accepted the gesture graciously. I kissed her cheek and sat with Ian.

The celebrant talked about Dad's life. None of it resonated with me. I sat clutching Ian's hand. We both shed a few tears.

My tears were about the fact that we never really connected properly, and we had missed out on *what could have been. But we all did our best.*

I didn't know what Ian was thinking. I didn't want to pry.

We all moved on from the church to the crematorium. Ian and I were given spaces in the funeral cars for this journey. A nice touch. We totally weren't expecting that.

Once we were all inside, I found the right moment to put my request to Irene to ask if I could say a few words.

"Irene, I would like to say a few words, is that OK?" I asked, timidly.

She was surprised, but she maintained her composure.

"Yes, OK dear. There's no room for nonsense, though. I'm sure you will be respectful."

I understood why she said that, completely.

Despite me '*doing my best*' over the years, I wasn't exactly the easiest to get along with. It couldn't have been *all* her fault we didn't get on…

I had to take responsibility.

"I want to thank Dad and I owe him an apology," I said, hoping to reassure her. I didn't want to add any stress to an already difficult day.

She nodded.

I liaised with the celebrant, who happily gave me a slot in the running order.

At the allotted time, I stepped up to the podium and spoke from memory. I needed no notes or prompts. It was crystal clear, what I needed to say. I began:

"I wanted to say a few words about Dad, because I feel I owe him an apology. You see, we didn't have an ordinary relationship. It was complicated. I only lived with him until I was five. I didn't spend a lot of time with him after that. In his absence, I wished that my dad could be *what I wanted him to be*.

I've always been a fan of a TV programme with a great personality: *The Val Doonican Show*. To me, Dad looked a lot like Val Doonican. I think it was the hair and the teeth that did it. More than that, in my mind, my dad was *like* Val Doonican. In that gap where Dad was missing, I made up the person I wanted him to be. I modelled him on Val. However, when I did spend time with Dad, he was not much like Val Doonican at all! He couldn't sing for a start, but actually he was also a very different kind of person. Dad would always disappoint me, because he was not like Val. I'm sorry, Dad, for setting you up to fail in that way. I think it was a coping mechanism.

I also wanted to say thank you to Dad for making me who I am today.

After hours of counselling and therapy I am now able to say that I am an OK person. I'm only the person I am today because of the life I've lived.

Not living with Dad has had its advantages.

Because I wasn't able to need my dad, I am very independent. I've never been able to rely on him, so I have learned to rely on myself. For that I am truly grateful.

Because of the type of parent Dad was, I have chosen to be the type of parent I am today. I grew into a parent who made deliberate choices about how to be. Without that experience, I doubt I would be the parent I am today. I have two wonderful boys with whom I have wonderful relationships. I thank you, Dad, for that.

Because of my struggle with not feeling valued as a person, having low self-esteem growing up, I have learnt a great deal about self-worth to help myself. Low self-esteem was a challenge for me in life. Because of that, I have made it my business to learn about coping with this. This has not only helped me, but it has also helped me in my business life. In my coaching work with my business clients, I have been able to use my experiences with others who faced the same battle with low self-worth, there is a lot of it about! I truly thank you, Dad, for that gift. So do all those people who have benefited and will benefit from that in the future, too. I'm sure of that.

By giving me nothing, Dad, you gave me everything I needed. I thank you for that. I loved you very dearly."

Almost everybody in the room clapped as I sat back down and took hold of my brother's hand.

It felt good to say that. At that moment I realised all the struggle had been worth it.

I finally came to a place of knowing that I didn't need my parents to want to spend time with me anymore. I just needed to fully appreciate how to like myself for the person I had become, because of the life experiences I'd had.

I needed to find gratitude and acceptance, to cease the resistance of what is, in order to end the suffering I was putting myself through.

I needed to spend some time with me.

PART TWO

I embarked on a new path, prompted by my values and a drive to make things better.

I felt enraged about the lack of good leadership in my working life and started a journey towards learning about the *best* way to lead people.

What follows in the second part of this book is a summary of my learnings and helpful tips and techniques to help you improve your transformational leadership skills.

I'm sharing what I have discovered in my personal growth journey. These chapters take you through models, theories, techniques and experiences which will help you transform the way you lead.

My aim is to capture the essence of my discoveries and to inspire you on your journey into transformational leadership.

In Part Two, I share my learning with you. I hope you feel moved to become a transformational leader.

The world needs you now more than ever.

CHAPTER NINETEEN
LEAVING ONE COLLEGE, LEAVING THE NEXT, STARTING MY OWN BUSINESS

Have you ever thought about that pivotal moment that got you to where you are now?

Is there one moment in your life that changed everything forever?

Here's mine:

I'm making up the names for the purposes of disguising them, but what follows is an accurate and true account.

My pivotal moment came shortly after the day one of my BTEC students asked me why I didn't have my own business, and, at the time, things at work were becoming fractured.

The impact of the merger between the Sixth Form College and the FE College became more evident. The huge disparity between different terms and conditions for teaching staff from the two sites was, by now, a thorny issue. The board were obviously looking to downgrade pay rates, not upgrade.

Industrial action, heated debates at staff meetings, changes to contracts, restructuring, OFSTED, student numbers, changes to the curriculum, new qualifications coming in and recruitment problems were just a few of the matters causing strife.

The classic 'culture clash', which is a common characteristic of any merger between two organisations, added fuel to the fire and bred a serious case of 'them and us'.

On a busy day in June 2009, I walked over to a meeting. I had an apprehensive face and a heavy heart. (Not from the POTS, but simply because everything had changed, and it was hard to see what had improved. The endless meetings ate destructively into precious teaching time. We all resented it. As I often tell people, "You can't hold love AND resentment in your heart.")

Clutching my meeting paperwork under my arm, I trudged across to the other side of the site, en route to the bland office block, to join the combined management team meeting.

The atmosphere had deteriorated to such an extent in my building that we secretly called the other building The Dark Side, but please don't tell anyone I said that!

The drab office décor of grey and corporate blue added to the oppressive atmosphere of the board room. Dominating it was the huge, shiny table, surrounded by the opposing teams – it was tense.

The chill in the air wasn't just down to uncomfortably cool wafts from the air conditioning. It was the lack of warmth in the new, poorly developing relationships between the two teams.

The chairman of the meeting (let's call him Brendan) was posturing. He adjusted his tie, jutting his chin forward and back to wriggle free from his tight-fitting, sweat-stained shirt. (Imagine a slightly chubbier Alan Sugar, and that's Brendan to a tee.) He was in full flow, pontificating. The future ethos of the merged organisation was being spat out, and I felt rage building within me.

I tried to suppress it, surreptitiously taking deep breaths, but failing miserably. My chest rose and fell more rapidly as he continued to spout.

"You see, you guys just don't do it our way," said Brendan, jutting his chin towards us. "We're not opposed to a bit of bullying and intimidation, because it works. The results speak for themselves. You can't argue with that."

He cast his eyes around the room and across to his team and they visibly shrunk in their seats.

I couldn't hold back any longer. Deliberately trying to remain calm and controlled, I had to interject.

"So, can I just check that, Brendan? You've just said that your preferred leadership approach is bullying and intimidation. To rule by fear?" I asked, looking around the room, noticing the crumpled body language of the managers from 'the other side'.

"Do you mind if I just check in with your team, here, to hear what they have to say?" I continued, whilst trying to supress the tremble and the rising tone in my voice caused by the rising wave of injustice.

Brian, the gaunt-looking, grey-haired Premises Manager (only 42, but looking more than 55 in his faded blue, company-issue work wear, with his cheap tie, scruffily dangling across his chest), sunk further into his chair as I caught his gaze.

Miriam, the Support Services Manager, in her neat tweed suit and her highly-coiffured, brunette hairdo, looking terrified at the thought I might ask her to speak. She twitched and fidgeted in her seat, looking everywhere but at me.

However, Adam, the Marketing Manager, with his strong bone structure and smart, crisp, white shirt, leaned forward. He said, "Yeah,

Rachel. It's pretty awful, actually. I can't keep any staff for longer than two weeks. No one with any decent skills applies. The quality of the work is really poor, because everyone's too busy looking over their shoulders and worrying about what's coming next. People are paralysed with nerves most of the time. I'm sick of it. I hoped things would change after the merger, but it's just got worse. Now there's all the restructuring on top on that. Everyone has got to apply for their own jobs! It's ridiculous!"

Without delay, Brendan jumped in to respond. His voice booming aggressively, he leaned towards Adam and bellowed, "Well, it's about choices, Adam. You either get on here, or get out!"

I'd had enough by then.

I stood up, my knees trembled a little. I attempted to step out from my seat and place the chair neatly under the table. Brendan raised his eyebrows at me. Before he could speak, I cut him off.

"I've made my choice, Brendan. I choose not to compromise my values and stay in this meeting with this unprofessional behaviour. In fact, I've made my choice to remove myself from this new management ethos altogether. This is not for me. I'm leaving this meeting and leaving the college. Please excuse me."

And with that I left.

In that meeting, in that moment, I made a decision that would affect the rest of my life.

I *did have* a very successful management career spanning eight happy years at the Sixth Form College. I dedicated myself to my work and the people in it, students and colleagues alike. I couldn't help my personality drivers, or my values.

I gave my heart and soul to the organisation that was being dragged into something I could not be aligned with. I could not compromise my values.

I walked away from that meeting, back to my office and I don't mind telling you that I cried.

"What have I done?"

I was the main earner for my family and I had just walked out of a really good job *with lots of holidays that I could spend with my children.*

"What will I say to Neil? What am I going to do?"

But I could not stay there. I knew that conflicting my values so dramatically was adding to my chest pains.

I was called into the Principal's office to discuss my behaviour. There followed a frank exchange of views. He accepted my resignation.

I knew I wasn't ready to start my own business yet. I had not done all the preparation. I had not learnt enough, and I hadn't asked Neil about that yet, either!

Fortunately, at that time (2009), there were lots of good management roles in education, because people were leaving the sector in droves.

I told Neil that I wanted a change and he supported me in that decision. He knew that I couldn't be there under that regime, and I wasn't the kind of person who could hide my truth. I had to live it.

I spotted a role similar to mine in the neighbouring town. I applied and was recruited.

"Thank goodness for that," I thought.

In Autumn term, 2009, *I jumped out of the frying pan and into the fire.*

I moved from one organisation, which I thought was deteriorating badly, to another organisation, which was an absolute nightmare! My new job made the old job seem like a dreamy place to work. The senior management were the biggest bullies I had ever encountered in my life! *Awful*. I hated the building, but the students and my fellow teachers were lovely. (Two of the most wonderful people I worked with in that dreadful place were Vicki Wilken and Pru Blackwell. They both left and started their own businesses, too. They encouraged me to start mine. I am extremely grateful to both of them.)

This seemingly wrong turn along my career path was actually a significant blessing. It convinced me, more than ever, that I had to do something important. It reaffirmed my belief that I could not stay where I could not align myself to the values. This crucial piece of learning spurred me to study leadership.

So, for three years, I buried myself in learning and development. (I am always learning and developing.)

Then I set up my own Leadership and Management Business Coaching Company.

CHAPTER TWENTY
TWO TYPES OF LEADERSHIP – WHICH ONE GETS RESULTS?

I made the decision to become self-employed and launch my business to showcase my interpersonal skills and apply all my learning and experience.

My first action, after having my logo designed and business cards printed, was to join the local Chamber of Commerce. Then I found myself a business coach. If I wanted others to have one, then surely I must have one myself! I became a member of the Entrepreneurs Circle and worked with Dan Bradbury in his group coaching offer. The only issue I had was that I did not have the income to pay for these things, yet, so the investment had to go on my credit card! I needn't have worried though, because within the year I had a bunch of great customers and a good reputation. The business grew after that, and I created a good income. The other bonus was that I could choose when I could sit down! This helped me massively with the fainting!

I launched officially at a local Business Expo. Armed with leaflets, a table, business cards, a roll-up banner and a smart suit, I threw myself into looking for customers. I had learnt all about marketing and sales over the years and now I was applying my learning. Luke came to help me set up – I thought it would be good experience for him. Joe wasn't available.

As coached to do so by my heroes at that time, I made a list of the 100 customers I thought I could help best and went about approaching them.

In those first months I carefully chose the types of people I wanted to work with and did not charge them much. I asked that if they found benefit from my services that they provide a review/testimonial. I wanted to build a great reputation. In my mind I had little credibility and needed to prove my worth at that point.

I attended hundreds of networking events, having read a brilliant book by Allan Pease, *Questions Are The Answer*, about how to have great conversations with other people and to find out whether your services match what they need. Another great resource for any business owner, in fact anyone at all!

My main objective for my business was to be the 'go-to' coach for business growth, and to support business owners and leaders to be brilliant at leadership. I genuinely wanted to help people. I've gained so much by truly wanting to be of service. People can spot a fake miles away.

I was on a mission to help create transformational leaders, because I genuinely believed that it could help grow the economy. Having left the education sector, I was still holding the students in my heart and wanting to make sure they all had somewhere to build a great career.

But, what's the difference between *transformational and transactional leadership?*

Here is a summary of what I learnt.

I had previously watched in dismay as frustrated employees left the two merged educational organisations where I had worked. Many of the senior leaders didn't understand the power of coaching, or failed to act to make the necessary changes towards it. It was so unbearable, I had to leave. So did many others.

Many successful classroom teachers are promoted to management positions, never having been out of the education system. Suddenly they have to move away from their strongest skill set and into the zone of managing adults and the quality of work other people deliver. It's a pattern often repeated in all sectors of the economy. Honestly, how many senior leaders do you know who have actually had training to manage people?

Transformational leadership began life back in 1978 when James McGregor Burns wrote his powerful book: *Leadership*. One of the most significant concepts was that, *"…leaders and their followers raise one another to higher levels of morality and motivation."*

In 1985, further work by Bernard M Bass in his book, *Leadership and Performance Beyond Expectations*, took the next steps and built the model I am so fond of today.

A ***transformational leader*** has these characteristics:

- Is a model of integrity and fairness.
- Sets clear goals, has high expectations.
- Encourages others.
- Provides support and recognition.
- Stirs the emotions of people.
- Gets people to look beyond their self-interest.
- Inspires people to reach for the improbable. Leadership is

proactive.

- Works to change the organisational culture by implementing new ideas.

- Employees achieve objectives through higher ideals and moral values.

- Motivates followers by encouraging them to put group interests first.

In contrast to this, an alternative view Bass explored was of that of the ***transactional leader***. He based this on earlier work first described by sociologist Max Weber.

The transactional leader's characteristics were described as being based on the following assumptions:

- People perform their best when the chain of command is definite and clear.

- Rewards and punishments motivate workers.

- Obeying instructions and commands of the leader is the primary goal of the followers.

- Subordinates need to be carefully monitored to ensure that expectations are met.

- Leadership is reactive.

- Works within the organisational culture.

- Employees achieve objectives through rewards and punishments set by leader.

- Motivates followers by appealing to their own self-interest.

To create the best results for an organisation, leaders need to bring out the best in their employees. I've seen many times how the more 'old-fashioned' approach of a transactional leader can get results – BUT ONLY WHEN THE LEADER IS PRESENT to enforce the *discipline*.

(I'm reminded, here, of the plumper Alan Sugar look-a-like from my previous chapter.)

In a culture where transformational leadership has evolved, the engagement of the staff is much more deeply rooted. Staff feel empowered and motivated. The mark of good leadership is what happens *when the leader is not there*!

Think about organisations and leaders with whom you are familiar. What do you know about the leadership style? What happens in the leader's absence?

What I truly love about transformational leadership and the principles listed above is the significant shift from the importance of 'I' to the power of 'we'.

In one business I worked with, this was the dramatic shift we all observed.

We started with a programme for the Board of Directors to set out the vision (see Chapter 22). There was a divide. There were challenges around unrequited love. (It happens!) The impact had leaked all across the business like toxic fumes. The bitterness was destructive. It was as if the rejection felt by the spurned lover was contagious.

The board urgently needed to be reunited. I can't say too much for fear of giving away the company and revealing secrets I am sworn to keep! Suffice to say that this huge company with a £250m turnover and 10 outlets had some healing to do. The culture was deteriorating at a time when the market was being disrupted by dramatic online developments by the competition.

Putting the hurt egos aside was essential. The way to do this was to build a shared future. In a series of intense group sessions and even more intense 1:1 coaching, it was possible to build a true sense of 'we'. I doubt this would have been possible with a transactional style of leadership. The MD made an excellent job of building and sharing the vision. Everyone was lifted by the sense of fairness and integrity, and there was a huge emphasis on recognition.

The atmosphere gradually changed, and each member of the board developed a sense of a higher purpose. This spread across the whole staff. It was truly uplifting to be a part of that change process.

How can organisations make the change to transformational leadership?

There are four steps:

Step 1: Create an inspiring vision.

Step 2: Motivate people to buy into and deliver the vision.

Step 3: Manage delivery of the vision.

Step 4: Build ever-stronger, trust-based relationships with your people.

Those organisations that do this are the ones having massive success and creating outstanding results through expert leadership.

Staff engagement and retention improve significantly within six months of the change. Trust-based relationships take longer to build, there are bridges to mend. Over time, there is a significant improvement in quality outcomes across the entire systems and processes of the organisation.

There is something significant to say at this juncture.

There is a place for ***transactional leadership***. It suits certain situations, for example in an immediate emergency.

When the speed of a decision is paramount, then you may need to be transactional, for example to save a life.

Certain industries with a particular style of work, and a particular profile of employees, may find that transactional is more effective. I would need to see the evidence and to know that other methods have been tested and ruled out before I agreed.

My experience of working with smaller businesses wanting to grow informs me that *everything happens as a direct result of leadership*. This includes great results, brilliant projects, winning prizes and much more. However, it can also mean high staff turnover, poor financial control, lost opportunities and worse.

Taking time to develop great leadership skills is a crucial part of building a great business.

More recently, my learning has included following the work of Mary Portas and the emergence of the **Kindness Economy**.

I attended the excellent ActionCOACH BizX Conference in April 2023, where Portas was a keynote speaker. She moved me to explore what is happening in this area and how this links with the work I do. (By the way, you won't go wrong if you attend one of these highly impactful ActionCOACH conferences. I'm not on commission! I'm just a fan of a fantastic learning event.)

I am delighted to see that the developments taking shape in more forward-thinking businesses mean that transformational leadership is re-emerging as the way forward. All the principles in both align perfectly. Portas' book, *Rebuild*, outlines the overlap/alignment clearly – check out the table on page 49 of her work. Right there at the top sits exactly what I am so passionate about.

The shift she describes of moving away from an economy based simply on growth and profit (*and sod the consequences*) towards the necessity of the shift towards The Kindness Economy is shown as two columns – highlighting the AND.

Here are a few examples:

Growth Economy	**Kindness Economy**
Me Me Me	Me AND We
Financial Growth	Social AND Financial Impact
Hard Skills	Hard AND Soft Skills

(Portas 2021, p49).

I simply love everything Portas has to say about the economy, business and leaders. In my view she should be in charge of the country. The world, even. She cuts right through the crap and into the heart of it all.

What is really great about *Rebuild*, by Portas, is that it gives you ideas you can act on immediately to make an impact. I was so inspired that I began a new habit. It's simply this: every time I go shopping I change one more product over to an environmentally friendly alternative. I'm a much more aware consumer. I'm now 'buying into' not just 'buying'. I hope it catches on. She advocates incremental changes in aspects of business to effect change for the better, for a higher purpose, i.e. for humanity as a whole. What's not to love?

Another significant point to add here is that the younger generations are really into working for 'switched-on' companies. They want to find *meaning and purpose*. Portas is great at getting this across in *Rebuild*.

Read these again:

Transformational leadership involves these principles:

- Inspires people to reach for the improbable. Leadership is proactive.

- Works to change the organisational culture by implementing new ideas.

- Employees achieve objectives through higher ideals and moral values.

- Motivates followers by encouraging them to put group interests first.

We are facing so many issues as a species. Let's face it, if we aren't careful, we could all be doomed! Something has got to change and business leaders are going to have to get on with it, or there won't be any customers left on the planet!

No wonder younger people feel overwhelmed, and many of them have anxiety. (On that note, loads of middle-aged and more mature people are feeling the same.)

They want to be part of the solution.

They won't respond well to transactional leadership, unless they choose a life in the armed services. They want something better, because they want to build a better future.

On this note, I feel proud of both my grown-up boys. Both of them would only choose to work for ethical companies. Joe even looked up the investment profile of his future employers. He noticed that one prospective employer had investments in diamond mines, and not the good type. He withdrew from that application and committed to applying his skills and abilities to a worthy company. (Proud mum alert, both boys have first class honours degrees. Luke in Music and Joe in Physics. I love those boys.) Both boys feel the same about this and I think many *aware* young people realise the significance of the values of an organisation. People say 'woke' and 'snowflake'. I say 'awake' and 'concerned'. (It could be more than concerned. It could be terrified about the future.)

Someone has got to be. In fact we all ought to be lifting our heads out of the sand and facing up to doing the right things in the right way. That's basically what transformational leadership is about.

Once I realised that this leadership concept underpins everything else, I was up and running.

Exercise:

Think about the times you have been inspired by somebody.

Reflect on what it was that moved you.

Can you link this to your own values and beliefs?

CHAPTER TWENTY-ONE
THE INSPIRATIONAL LEADER

How do you go from being *operational* to *inspirational?*

What does it mean to inspire someone, anyway? If you think of a time when you have been inspired, what did it make you feel?

When I ask people this in training sessions, they often say, "I felt moved."

> "Without inspiration, the best powers of the mind remain dormant. There is a fuel in us that needs to be ignited. Fortunate is the one who has the person with the spark around them to ignite their fuel."
> **— Johann Gottfried Von Herder**

I absolutely LOVE this. Are you someone who can be that spark for others? Can you ignite people? All leaders are this, if they are doing leadership correctly.

Leadership is movement. One human being interacts with another, or a group of them, and as a result people and things move. Hopefully, they move towards something better. It is very hard to move people towards something which is worse! That's basic human instinct.

> Inspire: – verb, to inspire, to spur on: impel, motivate. Threats don't necessarily inspire people to work. b. : to exert an animating, enlivening, or exalting influence on. From the Latin *spiriture* – to breathe.
>
> **— Oxford English Dictionary definition**

To lead you need to 'breathe life into people'.

And that's leadership right there!

If you are a leader, then you have followers.

I did a massive amount of research on this topic when I started thinking about setting up my own business, and continue to do so. The most significant factor I kept discovering was *trust*.

Trust is a huge part of whether somebody will be inspired by you, and subsequently choose to follow you.

My colleague Dr John Blakey has dedicated his first book and his PhD to in-depth research, so rather than steal his thunder I highly recommend you study his book: *The Trusted Executive*, and check out the charitable foundation he has set up, The Trusted Executive Foundation, the not-for-profit organisation he established to help change the world.

I am honoured to be working with him. There's a man who lives his values.

Why would anyone choose to follow you if they didn't trust you? Trust is the first building block of inspiration.

It's also very difficult to feel inspired if somebody isn't optimistic around you!

The two things go together. Interestingly, I said to my eldest son, Joe (who is a fair way along the Autistic spectrum), whilst conducting my research and doing the learning to set up my business, "Optimistic people live longer."

A couple of weeks later he said to me, "Mum, you told me that pessimistic people die younger."

Perception is everything.

How you see the world affects everything you do and everyone around you.

What do you see when you read this?

'Opportunityisnowhere.'

If you see:

Opportunity is *now here*, then that's your optimistic focus being dominant.

If you saw:

Opportunity is *nowhere,* well, need I say more. See later chapters on how to deal with this one!

A big part of being able to inspire people is to have **energy,** and that energy comes out in your enthusiasm. People need to buy into that direction, that journey, that vision, and the way they can do that is by understanding what's in it for them, what they will gain, what the team will gain.

In order to be inspirational, one of the things you can use in your organisation, which is free, is the power of stories. Telling people stories to motivate them and inspire them, which are, of course, genuine, true and sincere.

In recent years, the power of storytelling has blossomed. We are hard-wired as humans to respond to stories. There is a whole industry dedicated to this. Podcasting has evolved as the perfect opportunity to tell stories.

My two favourite podcasts are:

- The High Performance Podcast with Jake Humphreys and Professor Damian Hughes
- The Business Excellence Podcast with James Vincent of Action COACH

I have had the pleasure of working with both Professor Damian Hughes and James Vincent. I highly recommend these two podcasts as great learning resources, and I am incredibly grateful for all their support.

Listening to people tell their stories is a powerful motivator, and telling true stories is part of building trust.

I've started my own Podcast (available in all the usual podcast places!) It is called Transform Your Leadership.

Stephen Covey, author of the book *Seven Habits of Highly Successful People* did vast studies into the habits of those people who have inspired others. He discovered that in his experience '...*significant distrust*' doubles the cost of doing business and triples the time it takes to get things done.

If we can build trust, therefore, it stands to reason that, if we have got *great trust in place of* distrust, we can reduce the cost of doing business and increase the speed of getting results.

Trust is like a performance multiplier, enabling organisations to succeed in their communications, interactions and decisions and to move with incredible speed.'

(Covey, 2004)

If there is only one thing you go and do as a result of reading this book, then it surely should be to **look at how you can enhance trust in your organisation.**

What *are* the things you are going to do?

When you've finished this book, if you haven't already explored Stephen Covey's *Seven Habits of Highly Effective People*, then I would recommend that's at the top of your to-do list. My view is that it should be compulsory reading for all leaders!

Straight after that I highly recommend that you read *The Trusted Executive* by Dr John Blakey.

Check out The Trusted Executive website. I am honoured to be an Associate Coach for The Trusted Executive. Honestly, I'm not on commission for any of these recommendations!

Exercise:

Access the free, downloadable Self-Assessment questionnaire about your own trust behaviours:
https://trustedexecutive.com/nine-habits-of-trust/free-resources/

Identify which of the nine leadership habits you feel you exhibit competently and those you feel need work.
Share your results with a close colleague or trusted advisor.
Spend time developing all nine of the leadership habits Dr John Blakey discovered in his research.

CHAPTER TWENTY-TWO
HOW CAN YOU LEAD YOUR TEAM TO BECOME WINNERS?

I LOVE the quote below about leadership because it is another way to sum up transformational leadership in a nutshell:

> "A leader is best when people barely know he exists. When the work is done, they will say, 'We did it ourselves.'"
> — **Lao Tzu**

There's more on this in Chapter 49, but don't rush off there just yet.

As a leader, your team's success *is* your success. The mark of a great human being, in my eyes, is one who has helped many others to have success.

So, how do you lead to ensure this happens?

One of the common starting points, when working with new clients, is when the MDs or CEOs say something like, "Rachel, I really wish my team could be more successful and create the outstanding results I know they are capable of."

At this point I always ask them to describe what outstanding is. I also get them write down the ways that they demonstrate *every day* how *they themselves* are outstanding.

In the words of Ghandi, "You must be the change you wish to see in the world."

Or, to put it another way, you have to lead by example. It's a well-worn phrase, but it's true when they say 'it starts at the top'.

For your team to be outstanding, *you* have to be, too. You also need to know what outstanding is *exactly*. What have you done today that is outstanding? More importantly, have you really noticed anything outstanding in your team and praised it? What did you do when you noticed something that wasn't outstanding? What happened then?

Everything comes back to the values. It's no good having a poster in the reception that states proudly what the company vision is and what the values are, if you, yourself, are not demonstrating the exact behaviours that manifest the values.

I've been to a fair few companies where they proudly display all the right stuff on their website, in the board room and all around the company, but when it comes down to it, nobody, not even the leaders (or MD or CEO) actually *lives the values.* Creating a winning team relies on a set of behaviours, which must be demonstrated right from the top of the organisation.

The most successful organisations do this. The best leaders live this. The best teams live it and are true to it.

There is more to come on vision and values later.

But, what about something more practical? What else does it take to have a successful team?

Well, the next ingredient is closely linked to those first two bits. Along with leading by example and living the values comes *alignment.*

It's almost too obvious to state it, but I will anyway (in case, as sometimes it's the obvious things that get missed!). When a team has a clear plan (assuming they do have this. Some teams don't and they don't stand a cat in hell's chance of winning without one!), there is at least a direction.

With a clear plan, comes *clarity.* It can be set out with a big fanfare and a 'bit of a do', or it can be simply disseminated without a fuss, but it must be set out. The real key is to keep up the effective communication about the team's progress and to gain **alignment**.

As my coach James Vincent often reminded me, "There is power in clarity."

(I am not a huge fan of the connotations of the word 'power'. In this sense, it means strength, not a controlling sense of power, not like a power-crazy dictator.)

Effective communication is time-consuming. It is an art. Nobody has ever mastered an art by accident or left it to chance. True *mastering* takes effort, but the rewards are high.

Communicating your vision is fundamental if you want others to trust you enough to follow you.

It's really hard to communicate effectively if you haven't written your plan down.

Writing a plan can be frustrating, and a dusty old document tucked away in the filing cabinet will not support a team to become winners! It needs to be a *living document* that is part of the fabric of everyday life.

You will undoubtedly need to amend it, so it's best to keep it handy and, most of all, to refer to it regularly.

People need to be able to refer to it, check in with it, amend it when necessary.

You might be thinking this is not rocket science, it is obvious so why have I spent time writing about it?

The reason is because so many businesspeople I have encountered in my 13 years as a coach never had a direction, or a plan, or anything to guide them through their activity each day.

They just do stuff in a very busy way. Being busy feels good and it is a trap one can fall into all too easily.

The model I sometimes use when coaching business teams to get a direction and build alignment is the *Best Year Yet* programme, based on the superb book of the same name by Jinny Ditzler. The principle of alignment is a key factor in bringing a team together to achieve the plan, i.e. to win.

Ditzler states, "Unless the behaviour and direction of everyone in a team is aligned with its plan, the energy will go in all directions with nothing changing. People may be saying all the right words, but the power is disbursed and the results are continually disappointing." (Ditzler, 2001).

I was honoured to be an associate at New Level Results with Simon Teague and Andrew Duncan. The investment in my personal development with Simon formed a solid step forward in my coaching journey and enhanced my expertise further. The Best Year Yet coaching programme's specific intellectual property for using this coaching approach belongs to New Level Results. As Steven Covey says, "Sharpen the Saw". It's habit number seven in that great book, *Seven Habits of Highly Successful People* – so I did!

But you can read these books for yourself. I'm hoping I can save you time here, but I do recommend you read them.

Q : How do you get alignment?

A : ***With the power of coaching***.

At the heart of all successful teams in the world of sport you will find a fantastic coach. You, as the team's leader, should be that coach in your business. By keeping up the feedback loop you can say to people what they need to hear to step-up their performance.

One of my favourite quotes on this comes from Robin Sharma. He uses this wonderful phrase, ***"I have an opportunity for you to get to your next level of wow"*** . It is a bit cheesy and rather American (although he is Canadian), but it's the key to a winning team.

As a side note, here is something I've observed:

It is becoming very much more common place for a group of business owners to say, "Who is your coach?" Back in 2012, the same group might say, "What is a business coach?"

What is coaching?

Coaching is a process which brings about change for the better. Transformation, innovation, progress, solution, improvement, evolution – all these words which can be used to describe change.

All businesses experience change as a constant. By working with a coach, change is a managed process. Leadership is about change. As I have said before (it's kind of my catch phrase): All coaches are leaders, but not all leaders are coaches. YET.

I am a leadership coach and that means I work with business owners and key people in the business to support change. This means growing the business, but it is also about change in all its forms. It could refer to a change in personal effectiveness, for example, managing time more effectively or improving work-life balance. It could mean improving profit or something more intangible such as improving team dynamics in your firm. Coaching is a highly motivational experience, which empowers you to realise your maximum potential with dramatic results.

If you have a team, this is *the* most effective way to achieve great results in your business and for yourself.

What is coaching not?

Coaching is not telling or advising. It might feel odd not to lead by telling people.

Leading as a coach ensures that your team is clear on the goals, directing the right activity towards achieving them, taking responsibility for their own performance and checking in with a supportive person who will ignite their fuel, stretch and challenge them.

Coaching ensures that you lead by raising awareness and encourage people to take responsibility for their actions to ensure success.

It is highly motivational and has a massive impact on business results.

How does coaching work?

Here is an analogy from a coaching 'bible', a massively helpful guide to anyone heading into a leadership role: *Coaching for Performance* by John Whitmore, a coaching guru.

A tennis coach would not get a very good result helping a budding tennis star by constantly asking:

- Are you watching the ball?
- Why aren't you watching the ball?

The player would be defensive, angry or unaware of the errors he/she is making.

A skilled coach would ask other questions to make the player really take notice of what is going on, such as:

- Which way is the ball spinning as it comes towards you?
- How high is it each time it crosses the net?
- Does it spin faster or slower after it bounces?
- How far away is your opponent when you first see it spinning?

"This way the coach has compelled the player to watch the ball and take the action with heightened awareness. It requires a higher order response – requires focus/awareness. Answers are descriptive not judgmental. Provides opportunity for a feedback loop for the coach".

— **Whitmore 2002**

This is what working with a coach is like. The questions force you to become aware and to take responsibility which drives up business performance. It makes you a better leader. It enables you to learn more about running a business as well as having your own set of technical and/or creative skills.

It's fun, tough, stimulating, thought-provoking and very effective at helping business owners raise their game and achieve more in their business.

This is what great leadership looks like. A good leader asks great questions. I heard a quote attributed to Einstein about the skill of asking great questions which is this: Einstein reportedly said that if he had just one hour to solve a problem, he would spend the first 55 minutes working out what the correct question to ask is, then spend five minutes answering it.

I've learnt this is a good way to think about a problem. I'd even go so far as to say that the quality of one's life can be determined by the quality of the question one asks. It's not about knowing all the answers. It's about asking the right questions and remaining curious.

There is more on this in Chapter 27 where we dive more deeply into the best coaching to get working with.

Exercise:

Reflect on the way you currently lead.

Do you tell, or do you ask questions?

Do you rush in with the answers to the problems your team present to you, or do you respond with, "That's interesting, tell me more about that...?"

Could you respond with, "That's interesting, what have you tried so far?"

Try this and see what happens for a few weeks.

CHAPTER TWENTY-THREE
THE DIRECTIONAL PYRAMID, THE IMPORTANCE OF VALUES

I am often asked about how to make things happen and move a business or a team forward with a plan.

In my experience, the key is having *absolute clarity* about what you want your business to bring you, i.e. *knowing what you want*. (As Stephen Covey says, "Start with the end in mind".)

From this point you can work backwards to what you need to do today in order to get to that point. Work back, break it down into chunks to decide the activities you will do as soon as you leave the room.

Coaching often involves deciding on the outcome and then working back.

How you work this out and how you move towards what you want is based on many factors.

To help with this I like to use the *Directional Pyramid*.

(Note: I have tried to find a reference or a source for this, but sadly I can't attribute it to anyone in particular. I did not devise it myself. Someone out there owns this reference. I thank them, whoever they are.)

Firstly, start by drawing a large triangle on an A4 page, or A3 if necessary. Then divide the triangle up into chunks by drawing fives horizontal lines across it.

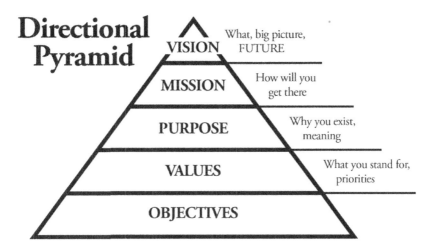

In order to get what you want from your business, you must spend time *identifying exactly what you want your business to bring you in the future.*

A good place to start is to think of a key date in the future. Avoid saying, "In 10 years' time".

This is not good enough.

If you pin-point a date, then calculate the number of months that equates to, you soon zone- in on clarity!

One of my clients, with a highly successful Electrical Contracting business, chose his 50th birthday. It's his ideal date. He wants to be completely out of the day-to-day running of his business, free from work, enjoying life, travelling with his wife. This provided utter clarity for us to work together.

If a client says "five years" I reflect back with, "So you have 60 months, or about 240 weeks." I ensure that we can actually articulate the date to see it clearly in his/her mind's eye.

This approach is trial and error, on occasions. Too much time for a person is not inspirational enough to create the desire to take action. Not enough time can create a sense of overwhelm.

What would be best for you?

Whatever is chosen must be entirely specific. For example, 31st August 2028. Not the end of summer 2028.

This part of the process is helpfully set out in the superb book by Jinny Ditzler called *Best Year Yet!*, as mentioned previously.

Jinny outlines the process, summed up below:

What do you want your long-term outcome from your business to be?

Push your imagination hard to 'see' yourself having already achieved your heart's deepest desires.

Since COVID-19, it is clear that *one thing for certain is uncertainty*!

However, think broad brush strokes here, at first. Then home in on the details. Safely imagine an ideal future in which you *already feel* highly satisfied.

Use the power of visualisation (like all elite performers do to prepare for any activity. This is no different).

So many business owners I've worked with have never actually stopped to think what *success* means to them.

Have you? What is it? Can you write it down?

My Electrical Contractor client is not driven by vast sums of money.

Not at all. He feels success when his apprentices move on and set up in business for themselves. When they do, he doesn't moan. He recruits some more! He has a queue of great candidates waiting to hear from him each year. He can pick the best of the best, because his reputation is one of training, support and mentoring. We worked together to help him identify that he sees himself as a centre of excellence for developing apprentices.

Success is different for everyone. If you don't have a clear idea of what it is, how do you know if you've reached it?

If you can't articulate it, how can you communicate with people who may need to help you achieve it?

If you can't be bothered to write it down, that tells me something.

The significance of writing goals down has been hotly debated since the growth of coaching from the 1980s onwards.

The only reliable source on the topic of the impact of writing down one's goals is an actual scientific study. Fortunately, one was conducted at Dominican University: the Gail Matthews Study, published in 2007 (not Harvard in 1953 – this study was a myth, although often quoted!)

The study recognises the value of writing goals down.

What does success look like, feel like, sound like, smell like for you?

When you have achieved it, what will you be saying?

What will others say about you and your business?

I urge my clients to capture this *visually*, either by hand drawing a physical picture, or creating one digitally. Some people hate doing this! But is it rather important.

Creativity engages more brain activity. It's about visualising the end point. ***When you can see it, you can move towards it***.

I'm asking the business owner, you, for your VISION – the place in the future which is better than now. I don't know anyone who deliberately plans to go somewhere in the future that is worse than it is here and now! The clue is in the word 'vision'. ***You 'see' it. That's why it is called a vision.***

Some people are not physically able to see images in their mind's eye. This is called *aphantasia.*

There is a huge amount of coverage all over the internet about the power of visualisation and its impact on success.

From April 2021 to September 2022, I was employed as a Business and Leadership coach by ActionCOACH. This world-leading, global coaching franchise was started 28 years ago by the serial-entrepreneur and billionaire Brad Sugars. He is arguably the single most successful business coach in the world.

His philosophy includes a Six Step Coaching Programme. One ingredient of which is the daily IVVM process:

Idealise – which means to have an idea.

Visualise – which means to see it in incredible detail.

Verbalise – to say it out loud.

Materialise – which means to bring it into being.

Brad affirms that the M won't happen without the IVV parts!

He hasn't done too badly on it!

I carry out this practice regularly and I believe it has helped me. So does Beyonce! (We're so similar!)

Here's my Vision:

- The Kindness Economy prevails
- People, planet and profit are valued equally

- Transformational leadership and trust-based relationships are paramount

Back to our pyramid – which, technically, is a triangle, I know!

Under the Vision is the **Mission**.

This is the journey. The *'how'* you will get there. It's best as a short, sharp, punchy statement of the way you will get to your vision.

For instance, RyanAir does this by cutting costs.

What will you do to reach your Vision? *How* will you get there?

So the **Vision** is the 'place and the what' in the future. The **Mission** is the 'how' you will get there.

Here's my mission:

- Coaching and inspiring leaders to make transformational change
- Increasing the number of B Corp Businesses in the UK
- Developing the nine characteristics of leadership which build trust-based relationships in all leaders.

A massive thing to be wary of here is that it does not work to just pay lip service to this.

Transparency is available and we live in an environment now which makes everything a company does visible. (Ask any restaurant or hotel who has received a bad review on TripAdvisor.)

You must not be fake, and you cannot over-promise and under-deliver.

You must do what it says on the tin.

Because you will get found out if you don't! (Portas is brilliant on this in *Rebuild.*)

During the Falklands War in 1982, it took six weeks for the video footage to reach the UK and get on to the news.

A Water Company discharges raw sewage into the River Thames and it is all over social media in the next 10 minutes.

Look at the P&O Ferry Company HR disaster, where the redundancies were made via a recorded video message at the beginning of the shift. The Six O'clock News was all over it by teatime.

I am all for transparency because it builds trust. My point is that writing your vision and mission and values cannot be simply a marketing exercise. It must come from the heart of you. ("People buy into you", remember. You are playing with people's feelings if you are not genuine.)

Under Mission is the **_Purpose_**.

Why does your business exist? If you were a stick of rock and I cut off your head, what would be running through the core of you as a statement? (Remember those sticks of rock, back in the days, when these were still a popular souvenir from the seaside?)

Back to RyanAir, they exist to make a profit by enabling as many people to travel as cheaply as possible. Reduce costs – go for volume.

As climate change surges more deeply into the forefront of our lives, they may well have to look at this. (It might no longer be appropriate to work towards this in the future.)

What's running through you, in your core?

If you cut off my head, you would see this mantra below, etched into my core:

All coaches are leaders, but not all leaders are coaches, **<u>YET!</u>**

That is why I get up in the morning. To help inspire leaders so that they can inspire others, so that everyone can have their best day at work being brilliant!

I want to leave a legacy of inspirational business owners who have moved into the Kindness Economy. I want to be part of the solution for the sake of future generations. I was going to retire this year, but after the session Mary Portas led at the ActionCOACH Conference in April I simply could not. There is important work still left to do.

What is your '*Why*'?

If you need help with your why, I highly recommend the inspirational work of Simon Sinek. His book *Start with Why* is a key resource here.

To get a flavour of his work in a nutshell, search Google for 'Simon Sinek, The Golden Circle'.

Here's a snippet from his website:

> "Very few people or companies can clearly articulate WHY they do what they do. When Simon asks WHY, he's not referring to making money—that's a result. Your WHY is your purpose, cause, or belief. WHY does your company exist? WHY do you get out of bed every morning? And WHY should anyone care about the work you do? When most organizations or people think, act, or communicate, they do so from the outside in (from WHAT to WHY). We say WHAT we do, we sometimes say HOW we do it, but we rarely say WHY we do it. But the WHY is the most crucial part of any endeavour or communication."
>
> **— https://simonsinek.com/golden-circle/**

Underneath your Purpose on the Directional Pyramid/Triangle are your *Values.*

This is the secret ingredient! Your *Values* are the most important bit of all. They lie at the heart of all activity. They drive behaviour. You make all your decisions within your *values framework.*

They are in your heart (figuratively speaking). They are what 'make you tick'.

They are built within you from birth. They are linked to your experience of the world, your upbringing, your family, your traditions, your education, your religion and beliefs, your influences in your environment, your experiences. There is some research being carried out into whether or not some of these are hard-wired in through genetics at birth. The jury is still out. Research is on-going, so the debate continues. By living by your true values, you will have *congruence* (alignment). You will develop a set of behaviours by which you stand and define yourself. You must be true to your values to offer sincerity, consistency, trust and a code of conduct that your customers, staff and other stakeholders will align themselves with, if they share the same values.

Remember, Mary Portas – "People buy into you, not from you"?

When your team or your customers match your values, or they at least hold them in high regard, because they believe in your vision, then you have the magic ingredient for getting great results.

Without knowing your values, how can you deliver these crucial aspects of your behaviour properly? Without living by them, how can you have congruence?

And, subsequently, without congruence it is hard to have happiness, and without this, it is hard to have success. See Chapter 37 for more on this.

It is a fact that wars have been fought defending values and millions of lives lost.

A common phrase people say is "being true to yourself". It means living by your values.

Your values define you and your business. They tell you how to make decisions. They guide you when making relationships. **Building a business is all about building relationships, after all.** Your values tell you what you *prioritise*. From this, you can identify your *objectives*.

Hang on a minute!

At this point I must mention *your brand*. You most likely realise that as a leader you have a personal brand, in addition to the company brand.

If I mention someone, say, Sir David Attenborough, and then I ask you to describe him in three words, you could. That's because he has a very clearly defined personal brand.

You have one whether you realise it or not.

When people talk about you behind your back, which they will do (of course, you are likely to be a boss if you are reading this), what three words do they currently say?

What three words would you like them to say?

It could be that you need to find a trusted friend to tell you what your three words are if you aren't sure.

Your values form part of your own **personal brand**, plus this will be the foundation of how you develop your **business identity** in your marketplace. It is that important. Dwell on your values and make them part of your business planning.

Remember Mary Portas and "buying into you" instead of "buying from you"?

So, to recap a moment:

From your values you can:

- Work out your priorities. This forms the basis of the objectives you will set yourself and for your business.

- This drives your purpose. Your purpose drives your mission and by driving this forward you will reach your vision.

- The vison is the bit at the end where you can say "We did this!" For my Electrical Contractor client, he will be travelling the world with his wife whilst his appointed MD runs his business, and he gets lovely messages from all his previous apprentices telling him how well they are doing running their own companies! Having a clear and shared set of values will enable you to set the right objectives to move everyone in your organisation towards the vision.

- Once you know this, you can identify the daily **activities** you need to carry out to ensure that the objectives are met.

- From there it all should fall into place (with the correct level of accountability, reviewing and remedial action of course! P.S. Having a coach helps you keep to these too!).

What I am minded to add here is another quote from one of my favourite inspirational philosophers, Lao Tzu (some believe that he may not have in fact been one person, but an amalgam of several).

I love this quote, it reminds me of Brad Sugar's IVVMs:

> "Watch your thoughts; they become words.
>
> Watch your words; they become actions.
>
> Watch your actions; they become habits.
>
> Watch your habits; they become character.
>
> Watch your character; it becomes your destiny."
>
> **— Lao-Tzu**

Ghandi used this too, although he adapted it, replacing 'character' with 'values', which is why I wanted to include it here.

In my experience you cannot underestimate the impact of a clearly defined set of values at the heart of an organisation.

The more explicit you are about what you stand for, the less likely it is that you will have to put up with what you can't abide.

Ken Blanchard (co-author of the excellent series *One Minute Manager* books) said in his excellent guide for all those aspiring transformational leaders, *Little Book of Coaching,*

"If you stand for nothing, you fall for anything."

It's true. I have seen this with my own eyes. Time and again, when you boil most situations down, the common denominator is human behaviour! It's not a surprise, because we are all just humans interacting with each other in the work situation, or in the world.

Explicit standards of what the expected behaviours are make it easy for people to comply or move on. They either get it straight away, because they are aligned anyway, or they are coached to come to a place where they believe something similar. Or they leave, or get the sack!

Where there is a misalignment of values, sooner or later, there will be conflict. (See Chapter 45 on how to handle a conflict successfully.)

That's why great companies (I mean truly great ones, not those which are just good at marketing) set their values out and actually use this code of behaviour to guide everything they do.

You might want to think about what you stand for. At this juncture I will flag up the significance of the Kindness Economy and how this is really taking shape and influencing buying behaviour. Thank goodness for that! We do all want a future for humanity, surely?!

Here's a story about a client I worked with between 2014 and 2016.

We started our work together by doing the activity at the top of this chapter (the Pyramid/Triangle).

We had to do this activity from scratch, because despite the vision appearing on the website and a copy of it on show in each and every room, only one person from the board of seven directors sitting in front of me that day could answer the question, "What is your vision?"

The one person who knew the vision was also the only person who knew what the values were, too. This person was the 82-year-old grandfather of the current MD. Granddad founded the company in the 1960s. Three generations were in that meeting and only the octogenarian knew what the hell they were working towards!

I started to dig a little deeper. They didn't know the vision, but did they know what the company stood for? What about the behaviours they were supposed to be inspiring, role-modelling, maintaining?

Probably by luck more than judgement, a couple of the board

members knew a couple of the key words on the posters without having to look.

I showed them their own poster, which listed the words they had selected (but were probably not living by).

So, I challenged them with a series of questions:

What are the behaviours that manifest those values?

What do you see?

What do hear?

What happens?

What does the value '*resilience*' look like? How can you spot it? How do you reward it?

What is NOT resilience? How do you challenge and support a lack of resilience?

Resilience was actually the first one listed on their values poster. None of them knew what good resilience looked like.

From that point on we knew we needed to spend time working on the behaviours.

Like many companies, they listed the values of honesty and integrity.

It is a seriously significant promise to make to say that you value honesty and integrity.

So, we went again with the questions. I pushed hard, because a branch manager had recently been caught stealing stock from the company. Ultimately, the buck stopped there in the board room. Did the thief steal because he knew that honesty wasn't truly valued?

What does honesty look like?

What behaviours were they prepared to accept?

They wrote a list of those behaviours, setting out explicitly what was acceptable and what was not acceptable.

The clearly defined behaviours are now stated in the staff handbook.

They explicitly form part of the recruitment process, right from the beginning.

They are part of the code of conduct for all managers and directors.

More than that, the board committed to actually living those behaviours, as role models and custodians of them.

It is part of their culture, and they are embedding it.

Funnily enough, progression towards the vision was made more quickly after a short period of change, where some people left and some new people came after this impactful session.

During this activity the board said: "We don't tolerate deceit."

I said, "OK then, you don't tolerate deceit. So what is deceit? Is it taking home a packet of paperclips at the end of the week, or a roll of Sellotape to wrap up your Christmas presents? As a leader doing that, you have effectively stolen a roll of Sellotape. What happens then if a member of staff does the same thing? Deceit, is deceit, is deceit, where is the line? So if you are going to put in your staff handbook that you do not tolerate deceit, you have to be true to that."

I then wanted to push it harder. I bravely ventured forward to challenge them on deceit.

"What if any one of you seven directors here today is having an affair…"

Nervous laughter rippled around the room.

"If you are prepared to say that one of your value statements is 'We do not tolerate deceit', then staff hear through the grapevine that a director has been having an affair, what does that do for the credibility of the director? What does it say about the truth of the values?

If you want to write that value down and describe the behaviours that manifest the value, you have to live it. The people in this room – *you absolutely have to live it.*"

We did the same hard work on the next value: Competence.

"What does competence look like? Have you got a clearly defined set of standards that dictate what the role is that you want a person to perform? People need to know what to do, AND know to what standard, how well. In the army, if the sergeant says 'jump' you say 'How high? Sir!' It's a bit like that. You need to have a process in place that outlines what the behaviour looks like. How does that competence show itself?"

We thrashed that out for every role in the organisation.

What the role was, **how** it manifests itself, **how well** it should be done, what good looks like.

This applies to the function of leadership and management, too.

In your organisation, if you are training leaders, training people in your team, you need to have a code. That needs to be stated explicitly. You need to write that down and it needs to be referred to.

It is key that everyone is able to challenge and support everyone. You need a culture that says, "Do I have permission to remind you of the code for that situation? This is because I am not sure that what has just transpired went according to that code."

This is where the culture of feedback through coaching comes in. If you can't challenge each other on it, how will that code be upheld? This requires a culture of trust (it is fair to say that at the heart of everything to do with leadership sits trust).

For those two key ingredients, character and competence, how much are you prepared to invest in your competence? How much are you prepared to invest in your capabilities? Do you live your values? How do you know you are living your values? What have you got to refer to that helps you to do that?

These two dimensions are vital for creating trust. Once you create trust you can then build inspiration. That's not the only ingredient, but it is the most important one and it must be there in place before any of the others can be effective.

At the foundation of trust is your own credibility. The credibility comes with that willingness to choose to take responsibility.

I worked in an organisation where the Chief Executive stood up and actually said, on a staff development day: "I don't trust nobody, me! Nope! I have trusted people in the past, and they have let me down, so I don't trust nobody. No, not me."

That is exactly what she said, and that organisation failed. Failed Ofsted. Couldn't get staff, couldn't attract students, had a culture of bullying. It wasn't the students that were bullying each other, it was the leadership team that was led by a bully, who was bullying members of staff, who then felt completely despondent and actually most of them left, after one or two terms.

What a criminal waste of taxpayers' money. All because of a lack of trust.

It was an incredibly toxic, unhealthy, terrible environment to be in and the reason being, that person wasn't prepared to trust. It starts at the top. Therefore, nobody trusted anything or anyone within that

SPEND TIME WITH ME

organisation. There is absolutely no way that that person could inspire people to create winning teams.

That is another one of those organisations that I had to leave. Honestly, I have stayed in some organisations! But I couldn't influence that one. I tried my hardest to influence it – absolutely. I threw everything at that!

I had to accept it and what was best for me and for my health was to not be there, and a lot of people felt like that.

One thing I particularly remember about that leader was the way the energy in the room changed when she entered it.

I was lucky enough to attend a seminar by Dr Tom Barratt, the author of a best-selling book *Dare to Dream*. (He is an internationally recognised expert on success psychology and leadership.)

I learnt one main thing I always carry with me. He asked a simple question and I make sure I teach this to all managers and leaders with whom I work.

I also have it ringing in my head whenever I go anywhere or meet someone.

He asked: "What do you fill a room with?"

When you come into the room, what happens? How do people feel? What is it you want to create? Is it optimism? Is it trust? Is it enthusiasm? Is it energy? Is it despair? Is it cynicism?

What can you do to create inspiration, when you walk into the room, to create the right energy?

Even if that means you have had a terrible day, but you have still got time to smile at somebody and ask how they are.

Not by being insincere, but by being bothered. By understanding how much that matters.

Do the simple things, right. Don't over complicate it. You know what the simple things are:

"Hello, how are you?" and "Thank you".

Be present. Listen carefully. Have the energy to focus. When someone is talking to you, take the time to be an excellent listener. If you are struggling to do that, then I would recommend Dr Tom Barratt's book.

There was an interesting article in the Telegraph in 2011 *by* Richard Alleyne. He wrote that:

> "…in 1985, one edition of the Daily Telegraph was as much information as a person 100 years previous would have been exposed to in their entire life."
> **— https://www.telegraph.co.uk/news/science/science-news/8316534/Welcome-to-the-information-age-174-newspapers-a-day.html**

That was before Netflix, Podcasts, WhatsApp, SnapChat, Instagram, LinkedIn etc.

If you think about it, sometimes you get that muzzy-headed feeling.

I have a friend who has a jewellery business and she said, "Sometimes I don't know whether someone has contacted me by email, whether they have rung me up, whether they have texted me, whether they have done a Facebook message, whether it is on my WhatsApp, Instagram, LinkedIn. I can't think, because I have so much coming at me, I am distracted."

Television is on 24/7, everything is happening at 100mph. Even when you look at an advert now, the shots change, about 40 seconds of light, it's like watching Jamie Oliver, you can't just look at the picture. Everything is happening a million miles an hour and it is very hard to focus.

No wonder there is a rise in the number of people with anxiety. Everyone is frantically trying to work out who said what and on which platform.

Sometimes being still and just listening effectively is something that we lack now in our society. We can be inspirational in the way that we do that.

Do you know what might happen if you listen more effectively? What might be the result of that? They do say the further you go up your organisation the more likely you are to not hear what you need to hear.

But also, if you are role modelling effective listening, what might happen?

Your team will do the same. Try it for a week and just see what happens. Be totally present with everyone with whom you come into contact. Connect properly with the other human beings in your life. I am sure you will notice the impact it has.

Exercise:

Do you know what your values are?

Try the activity on this website:

https://www.mindtools.com/a5eygum/what-are-your-values

Do you have a vision?

CHAPTER TWENTY-FOUR
THE ART OF LISTENING

How effective are you at really listening to the people involved in your business activity? Are you a level one or a level three listener? How will this impact on your success?

> "We have two ears and one mouth, so we should listen more than we say."
> — **Zeno of Citium, as quoted by Diogenes Laërtius**

This is a simple observation by Zeno, the founder of the Stoic school of philosophy.

Why are good listening skills so important? Well, it boils down to basic human nature. Ralph Nichols is known as the Father of the Field of Listening and established the International Listening Association.

He stated: *"The most basic of all human needs is the need to understand and be understood. The best way to understand people is to listen to them."*

How much emphasis is really placed on the true art of listening in your business? Or even in your family or friendship groups?

This is a simple truth which, if we all lived by it, would make the world an easier place in which to live and do business. The only trouble with simple things is that they are often the most easily overlooked!

The other complicating difficulty with listening skills (in addition to missing the obvious and simple fact that most people hardly ever consider how effectively they are listening) is captured by one of my greatest heroes, Steven Covey, when he says:

> "Most people do not listen with the intent to understand; they listen with the intent to reply."
> — **Stephen R. Covey, *The 7 Habits of Highly Effective People: Powerful Lessons in Personal Change***

My point is that effective listening is a skill which needs attention, as it can greatly improve your personal effectiveness and the level of success you have with your business (and your personal life!).

There are said to be three levels of listening (Laura Whitworth, Co-Active Coaching, 2010).

- Level 1 is about our *internal listening*, which is our awareness of ourselves. As information reaches us, we capture it and process it, asking, "what does this mean for me?" Many people only ever achieve this level!

- Level 2 is the skill of *focused listening*. This is where there is a sharp focus on the other person. You listen with *all* your senses. (It is great to be heard by someone who practices level 2 listening!)

- Level 3 is called *global listening*. Here you listen as though you were the other person and you have an imaginary set of receivers to enhance your awareness, including accessing your *intuition*. This takes great skill and determination to remain present.

In many businesses there is far too much emphasis on one half of the communication process: the sending out of messages. This happens at many levels; internally, externally and in everyday interactions between the humans involved.

I would argue that there should be double the energy and focus placed on the second half of effective communication: the listening, i.e. two ears, one mouth. By doing this you will understand the people in your business (internal and external) and this will be sure to produce improved results.

What process do you have to ensure that effective listening happens in your organisation, or in your own daily activity?

Exercise:

Spend two weeks making a determined effort to be a level 3 listener. Note how this impacts the quality of the interactions you have.

CHAPTER TWENTY-FIVE
ELEVEN LEADERSHIP SNIPPETS

1. Can leadership be taught?

A quick lesson from the *One Minute Manager*, Ken Blanchard:

Can you learn how to be a manager? There is always a huge debate about this. What do you think?

Ken Blanchard's series *The One Minute Manager* has been a massive success and comes highly recommended for any person taking a leadership role. If you have not yet read any of these great mini-books they are well worth taking a look at. They are quick, powerfully helpful and easy to digest.

My best piece of learning from the leadership-focused ones answers one of the most commonly asked questions I am asked when training leaders. They ask, "What's the best leadership style?" Many people get fixated with their *leadership style.* They worry what it is, what it should be, what one is best.

This is the thing, though, that the leadership style is not about the leader. It is most definitely about *the person being led*. When I tell people this, they get confused. They always refer to a great leader they've known and they say that the particular style of that person was 'best'.

My answer is that a great leader has a style that matches the needs of the person they are leading. A great leader is able to adapt his/her style to match what will bring the best out in the person with whom they are working at the time.

Another way to think about this is to also consider the situation. What some situations require is diplomacy, tact, a gentle guidance, coaxing and encouragement. Another situation will require a leader to be direct, decisive, fast and bold, for example in an emergency or a crisis.

So when thinking about leadership style, it's not always helpful to focus on a particular style and stick rigidly to it. You may have a preferred style with which you feel more comfortable and that is probably the style that suits you best when you are being led. However, it's best not to fixate on that and be determined that it is 'how you are'.

Of course, there does need to be a level of awareness about your own strengths and weaknesses. We can't easily be what we are not. We do need to be living our truth. But with greater awareness comes the ability to develop new techniques, new methods and learn lessons about what works most effectively and with whom.

In my research I found a great article by John Eric Adair.

Adair was probably the first to demonstrate that leadership is a trainable, transferable skill, rather than it being an exclusively inborn ability. In *Great Leaders* (1995) he suggests that, "The common sense conclusion of this book is that ***leadership potential can be developed, but it does have to be there in the first place… Leaders are not born. Leaders are made, and they are made by effort and hard work.***"

In other words, everyone has the basic seeds of leadership within them and how these are developed and cultivated will determine whether leadership qualities develop in an individual. It has been argued that *"...more leaders have been made by accident, circumstance, sheer grit, or will than have been made by all the leadership courses put together. Leadership courses can only teach skills. They cannot teach character or vision... The ingredients of leadership cannot be taught, however. They must be learned." (Adair 1995)*

From my experience, different types of people can make different types of leaders. I believe the best leaders use coaching skills when the situation lends itself to it.

2. How can a love affair make the difference to your business success?

There are many factors which lead to success in business. Being unique, being first, being the best. Hard-nosed businesspeople can sometimes miss a trick. Feeling love can make a huge impact. It's all about relationships.

No matter what your business is, what you do within it, every day, offers you an opportunity to show the world something special. You have the chance to leave people with ***an experience of you*** that can make a difference forever.

Your 'work', when in business, is to build relationships. Nothing happens in business without them. They are the cornerstone of everything else that occurs. It's all about showing people love.

The love you have for your particular area, be that a specific skill, product, process or design, should shine through all your activities and most importantly in the way that ***you connect with people***.

No employee will work at their best if they can't feel that

connection. I must point out here that I'm not recommending you form inappropriate relationships with employees! Not that sort of love! I am talking about the love for what you do, for what they do, for what you can build together.

Your clients/customers will want to feel loved and to experience responding with a love for everything they gain by spending money with you. If they are sincerely, truly appreciated for what they bring to your success then they will do that more often and tell everyone about it.

Humans need love. It's fundamental. Business boils down to relationships and communication.

Become superior at showing love and see how this impacts on your business. It must be based in truth. Don't be a pretender. There's nothing worse than a fake. But if you can find the love in you and show it to the world, you will see how this helps your business grow.

Over the last 13 years I have met many inspirational people who exude love for their work.

Connecting with that wonderful source inside, which binds all humans, is such powerful magic.

If you have fallen out of love with any part of what you do or how you do it, you might benefit from working with a coach. Something must change otherwise it might all start to unravel.

Love is the glue that binds us.

Let's face it, there is a lot we need to do to make the world, with its current challenges, a more enjoyable place to live.

Exercise:

Take a moment to reflect on what you truly LOVE about what you do.

Spend time on this because this is what will drive you onwards when time is short, pressure is high and challenges come thick and fast.

Examine your responses to these questions:

L

Learn: What do you learn from others around you?

Leave: What could you not bear to leave out of your work?

List: List the activities which bring you joy

Like: What activities do you like because you feel very capable?

O

Open: How open are you? How authentic? How accessible? How true? How interested are you in new ideas?

Over: How quickly can you get over a set back? How do you help your team do this?

Tze: "A leader is best when people barley know he exists. When the work is done, they will say 'We did it ourselves.'"

Obvious: If something is obvious, be curious. How often do you hear the words 'we always do it this way'? If this is not serving you, then check it out. There is great value in consistency, but there is nearly always a better way something can be done. How often do you check on something which seems obvious? How much autonomy do people have to suggest improvements?

Outcome: "Start with the end in mind" is one of the habits in the brilliant book by Steven Covey, *Seven Habits of Highly Effectively People.* How well do you clarify the outcome? What questions do you ask to break the steps down, to help plan the way to achieve objectives?

One: Is a dangerous number. See progression planning, earlier. How well covered is access to *mission critical* pieces of knowledge or tasks? What happens in the event of a disaster, or when someone leaves?

V

Value: What provides great value to your life from your work?

Virtue: What do you feel you demonstrate in your work that is virtuous?

Vows: What 'vows'/promises do you make to yourself about how you lead? And to others?

E

Energy: Loving what you do provides energy – how do you feel this energy? Where does it manifest? What does good energy look like to you?

Evolve: Is there anything that can evolve/change about your work? What small changes can you make each day to feel more love for what you do?

3. Are you an assertive leader?

Assertiveness is often confused with being aggressive. Are you getting it right?

So many people I have worked with have been afraid to be assertive, because they felt it is somehow 'not nice'. As a leader, assertiveness is a crucial element of being effective. Actually, all employees in an organisation need to get this right, otherwise it can have a very negative impact on the business, and I'm not just referring to poor customer service or an aggressive person on the end of a phone. It's also bad news if someone is too passive.

So, what is it like when you are being assertive?

A definition I like is taken from *Developing Positive Assertiveness – Practical Techniques for Personal Success* by Sam R. Lloyd, who says it can be defined as 'being confident to express your needs, thoughts/opinions and feelings in a considerate and respectful manner.'

This leads to clarity, fairness, productivity, respect and enhances a leader's credibility. It's the way to go!

That is definitely different from being aggressive! This can be defined as 'saying what you think, expressing your needs with **only self-interest**, with no regard for others' views or no respect for the other person. It includes using tone and body language which can be intimidating, inflexible and controlling.' (Lloyd 2001)

It is easy to see where aggressive behaviour can negatively impact a company. Typical traits of someone with aggressive behaviour can include losing their temper, being unnecessarily competitive, using threats or intimidation, being unwilling to listen to others' views, shouting, bullying and not asking for help.

These can all lead to poor results in an organisation, but it is still not unusual behaviour for some less developed leaders. It can also create a culture of fear, which badly affects how people perform (especially creative people). Under the stress caused by aggressive behaviour, the competency of the prefrontal cortex is impeded. That's the part of your brain which came last in human evolution. I'm no brain expert, but I have learnt a great deal about the brain.

Right now, throughout the world, scientists and experts are studying the human brain with increasing skills, technology and expertise. One thing is for sure, the more they find out about how the brain works, the more they realise there is much more to learn!

All in all, aggressive behaviour can affect a business very badly. Most significantly, the problem often only gets worse as most people become afraid to provide the feedback to the aggressive person that they need in order to develop and improve. It's a sad spiral of increasingly poor performance. It is one of the single most common issues in companies where recruitment and staff retention are problematic, for obvious reasons. It wastes so much money, time effort and opportunity.

Here is an important factor to bear in mind: There is always a reason why someone displays aggressive behaviour. There's more on that at the end of this chapter.

The other side of the spectrum is when passive behaviour becomes a problem.

Being passive can be defined as: 'Not saying what you think, feel or need. **Only considering others' views**. Not expressing your own interests/needs. Using body language and tone which are submissive, too flexible.' (Lloyd 2001).

A person with passive behaviour can show traits such as always saying yes and becoming overloaded, overworking and suffering burnout, not asking questions and spending time guessing what needs to be done, being paralysed with reasonableness, resulting in nothing getting resolved, being too eager to please whoever they are faced with and not necessarily helping a situation. This type of behaviour is less easy to spot, but can also have very damaging effects on a business. And on the person who is being passive.

A leader with passive behaviour can cause stagnation and confusion, as people lack direction and eventually lose faith.

The leader with passive behaviour habits is often seen as 'a waste of time' and can get bypassed. They can be seen as insincere. It's a very common occurrence when someone is promoted from within without a helpful level of assertiveness to carry out the new role.

On many occasions I have been asked to coach a team member in an organisation, because they did not feel able to be assertive.

An example of this was in a very busy medical treatment centre. The customers were often in pain, and checking in and checking out was stressful. The receptionist had to work to a tight schedule to keep patients flowing in and out smoothly. Appointment times were tight, and people were flustered when asked about making their next appointments.

From this experience I was able to develop a quick assertiveness check sheet. I thought it might be handy to share it here:

How to be assertive

1. It is all about having clear *boundaries*. These come from your job description and the objectives of your role.

2. In a difficult or conflicting situation, one in which you are required to be assertive, the first step is **to clarify what is being asked of you.** Feedback what you have understood – check or ask. Alternatively, you may be required to state something.

3. *Explain* clearly the situation from your perspective. Be explicit and link to the impact on your role and the work you are undertaking.

4. Never give a blunt, negative response. (*Never say 'No' outright.*) *Explain* what you *can do.*

5. *Explain your limits* (the framework is your job description, the objectives of the role).

6. *Remember: sometimes you cannot find a resolution alone. Seek support from another source.*

A helpful phrase is "What I can do is…"

I always remind people: "You have permission to be assertive. It is a healthy way to be."

I said it earlier: it's hard to hold love and resentment in the same space. Passive behaviour can lead to resentment. Learning to be assertive is always going to make you feel better in the long term. Overcoming the fear of being passive is a huge step for someone to take. With guidance and support, it is a skill which can be learnt and practised.

I'm definitely not a fan of aggressive behaviour. Not at all. But there is one good thing with people who display aggressive behaviour: *you*

177

always know what they want.

You might not, however, truly understand why they are behaving in that manner at the time.

My experience and all my learning in this area has led me to understand that scary people are scared.

An assertive leader will always try to understand what is behind the behaviour.

It is very often a reaction to feeling afraid of or about something.

That fear is generally fear of loss.

Loss can cover some or all of these (and many others):

- Loss of face
- Loss of acceptance
- Loss of status
- Loss of control
- Loss of identity
- Loss of money
- Loss of dignity.

You get the picture.

It takes a wholly secure person to cope with the loss someone else is afraid of.

4. Do you think about rubbish?

Are you a leader who understands rubbish?

The key thing to help a leader be more effective is knowing this one thing.

My mum always used to say to me when I was young, "You get out what you put in." I suspect someone, somewhere has said a similar thing to you, such as "you reap what you sow," or something along those lines.

It's easy to nod and acknowledge this and let it pass over you, because it is obvious on one level. However, the more I have studied leadership and coaching the more I realise this piece of advice is a gem!

I never fully understood my mum's brilliant words of wisdom until I worked with a number of different organisations as a leadership coach. Time after time I have had this lesson played out in front of me.

I've been lucky enough to spend time with Professor Damian Hughes. Damian is the author of six best-selling books, including *Liquid Thinking, Liquid Leadership, How to Change Absolutely Anything* and *How to Think Like Sir Alex Ferguson*. He is an expert in the psychological methods used by high achievers, and shows, in easy steps, how you can adopt them into your own life and business. He was the keynote speaker at the Leadership That Gets Results Conference I organised in 2015. He really brought it home to us all that day.

His morning session focused on this very lesson:

All organisations are based on the same idea. You take some ***inputs*** (such as labour, materials, entrepreneurial flair) and then you carry out a ***process*** to create some ***outputs. The thing at the end must have more value than the sum of the parts at the beginning. Otherwise, it's meaningless.***

You, the leader, are key to all of this as you are accountable for the whole of it. You cannot delegate accountability, but you can delegate ***responsibility.*** This takes huge levels of skill to do properly. (More on delegation in Chapter 31.)

It relies on the highly significant skill of *feedback*. Otherwise, delegation becomes abdication and then the whole thing goes belly up!

Using a coaching style of leadership is the one significant thing that can increase the chances of success, as coaching uses two main bits of kit to deliver results. The first being the skill of raising *awareness* in the people they are leading. The second is encouraging people to choose to take *responsibility*.

For this to work you, as the leader, need to have a deep understanding of what these two factors really are.

Awareness is: being conscious, not ignorant, having knowledge through alertness in observing or interpreting what one sees, hears, feels etc. (This is helped massively by you providing excellent feedback.)

Responsibility is: the state or fact of having a duty to deal with something or someone. This relies heavily on the coaching skills of asking the right questions of your people so that they *choose* their actions appropriately. The significance is in the *choice of taking responsibility* for process of improving. Without the *choice* there is no responsibility.

Let's dwell on raising awareness, because this is where it all begins. When you can create higher levels of consciousness and develop your people so that they are more alert to their actions and the quality of their work, the process improves and so do the outputs. So do motivation and innovation. They can only develop awareness when they are given feedback properly!

Here's the main thing: it is the leader's job to ensure that this awareness is at its highest in all their people.

The quality of the output depends on the quality of the input.
Here's the link to rubbish (finally!).

"Garbage in, garbage out." By becoming an expert at developing your people to spot garbage, as it appears at the beginning of any process, you reduce the risk of garbage coming out the other end.

This only works within a safe culture of feedback and with a coaching style of leadership. This transformational approach generates a culture of excellence and moves away from telling people towards creating a culture of taking responsibility. This all relies on heightened awareness.

5. The power of recognising good work

What impact does recognition of great performance or outstanding effort have?

Many leaders are reticent to deal with poor performance, as it can cause upset, and yet, at the same time, many leaders forget to notice achievements or great effort. This is a shame as the impact can be massive!

Here is an example of the power and impact of noticing good work and high effort levels from my own experience.

During my retail management career, way back in 1992, I was on a fairly good management salary for a person of my age and in an industry which was notoriously hard work and not great at rewarding staff. I was seconded to a project to multi-skill staff across a wide range of back office functions as a pilot for our region (which was subsequently rolled out nationally).

During those few months I was completely dedicated to the project and its worthwhile aims. It was intended to give more flexibility to the business, plus job enrichment and enlargement to staff. I was thoroughly enjoying the work and seemed to make a good job of it in a very good time. I regularly gave up my day off in the week to carry on with the task in hand to build on good momentum and high engagement from the trainees. I understood that I was NOT entitled to overtime, because of my management salary – despite that, I was working an average of 70 hours per week.

At the end of the project the District Manager (a short, rotund guy with a very wide parting, wearing a bland, grey suit) called me to the local store's management office and I thought that I had done something wrong!

I was really nervous when going in to see him. I sat opposite him in the dingy office, which was piled high with odd bits of stock and huge stacks of paperwork. To my utter surprise he proceeded to detail the improvements the project has already seen and to tell me how pleased he was with my work.

He noted how many hours I had been working and thanked me. I could not believe my ears! At the end of his speech I was unable to comment, because I thought nobody had noticed and they did not appreciate my commitment. I was stunned. I hadn't minded the hard work at all, because it had been a stimulating project and quite fun, too.

However, as I was about to get up out of my chair and to thank him for his time, he gestured that I should remain seated. He went on to say that the Head Office Team had considered that they couldn't pay me for all the hours I had worked, but they would like to offer me eight hours overtime *at double pay*.

I was completely blown away. It was literally unheard of for a manager to get overtime!

The fact is, I had worked at least 100 hours *for nothing* across the duration of the project, but the fact they were noticing my work was immense to me. This small gesture of some extra pay made the praise and recognition a bit more meaningful, but it was the gesture that mattered, not the amount.

My point is that by noticing this kind of extra effort or work that is done well and the context of it really had an impact on my sense of worth to the organisation. This happened over 30 years ago, but I can still remember the feeling today. I practically floated out of the office and glowed for months afterwards! I was even more highly motivated after that! Their investment in my overtime was a very wise one indeed.

Similarly, when I was studying at Brighton University and experiencing some very difficult personal and financial difficulties (when everything was rather challenging and the house was filled with students, babies and a sick husband!), the welfare office also noticed my effort and rewarded me with a grant from the Hardship Fund (great name! I wonder if it is still called that today!).

Someone noticed my effort and rewarded it. That made the difference. It helped me stay focused and to change my life. Someone noticed my effort to remain on task and rewarded me. It paid off, because I would not be where I am today if they had not thrown me that lifeline.

Most importantly, the fact that someone recognised that I had something to offer and wanted me to continue really helped me. I will always remember that! I feel now that I have been able to put my degree to good use, I want to encourage others to keep going and to never give up. I am not a millionaire, but I have improved my life, because someone believed in me enough to reward and support me when it was difficult. They recognised I needed that boost.

My point is to tell you as leaders to notice effort and to recognise good work, because the impact it has can last a long time and will make a huge difference to someone in your organisation.

6. Do you need to be ruthless to be a great leader?

Do you need to be ruthless and what does that really mean?

When I've worked with some leadership teams the word 'ruthless' sometimes pops up. Do you need to be ruthless as a leader?

That depends on what that means. It depends on where there is conflict. Dan Kennedy's great book *No B.S. Ruthless Management of People and Profits* explains this well. (Thanks to Nigel Botterill and the Entrepreneurs Circle again for an excellent summary, parts of which I'd like to share.) It's an interesting take on how to manage the people in your business.

Many business owners make the mistake of thinking that the people working for them care as much as they do about the business. The sad fact is that few rarely do. Your employees have their own personal objectives, which may not sit comfortably with the ones you have for them to achieve. There is potential for conflict here. Your employees can view you as an obstacle to them getting on with their lives!

Kennedy touches on the sensitive issue where another potential conflict can arise: if you have 'people pleasers' working in your business. He refers to the Willy Loman Syndrome whereby this 'common disease amongst failing sales professionals' causes them to have a powerful and overwhelming desire to be liked over and above the desire to make sales. Kennedy says it is a contagious disease and many leaders catch it!

If leaders are also 'approval seekers', it makes a huge and dangerous difference to their effectiveness. They can become paralysed with reasonableness, leaving them powerless to make a decision, and often – worst of all – to become insincere as they switch allegiances to the most dominant person influencing them at the time.

One particular guy I worked with comes to mind and most of his staff soon realised his vulnerability. They took to passing back up all unpleasant decisions to him, giving themselves a few more weeks before anything had to be solved. It was a massive time waster and caused everyone to lose the will to live when they needed an answer, but it helped divert the issue in the short term.

A great quote from Kennedy's book is, "There is no evidence whatsoever that a manager who is liked by employees creates more profit for the company."

Do you need to be liked to be a great leader? Kennedy obviously thinks not.

He predicts that Google's 'fun place to work' reputation is a fad that will see its demise. "The fact that Google has extraordinary profit margins, with no costs of manufacture and a never ending stream of revenue, hides lots of 'dysfunctional behaviour'," says Kennedy. He sees the day coming that the "…accumulated, out-of-control fat and waste and sloth will be slashed away by the 'hatchet man'."

To give you a flavour of Kennedy's emphasis on managing people, he asks the question, "How will you quantify the profit produced by an employee?"

It's a refreshingly frank view of the nitty-gritty of enterprise. I can't say that I agree with all that is contained in the book, but I can see the logic of looking at things this way. My personal view is that everything comes back to values and vision in leadership with a hefty measure of proper feedback and follow up.

7. The big leadership lesson at the Chinese takeaway, slow *is* fast with people

The seductive temptation that a takeaway offers can teach us all a crucial lesson in leadership behaviour. The glorious satiation of hitting that spot with what you crave! It's right up there. It's part of our culture in many ways. It is unusual to know of someone who has never experienced a takeaway food experience. Especially these days with all the delivery options available, you don't even have to move off the sofa!

Whatever your reasons for calling up for a takeout, you most likely know you will get what you want. Whether it's a late night rush to unexpectedly grab something quickly, or a planned social occasion with best mates round for a good night in, you generally are satisfied.

You use the suppliers you like best and they give you what you want. It is an exchange that works. In that moment, your desires have been satisfied. It's a fairly simple process that happens millions of times every day.

I love spending time investigating what works well and what does not. For most people, most of the time, the takeaway routine is an example of something which works well. If it didn't, you would stop using that provider. Think how disappointing it can be if you are expecting king prawn balls and you end up with steamed broccoli! So what is the key to this success?

The relationship between you and the supplier may not be a very deep one, but it is a successful one. You most likely hardly know the person at the other end of the line. But it works.

A common frustration I hear in organisations is when problems occur that result in a right old mess. Confusion, recriminations, blame, scapegoating, emotional baggage and much more all fall out of unsuccessful situations. I spend a lot of time working with excellent companies, but even then, there are always plenty of examples of when communication goes wonky.

Poor communication is the single most important factor in any unsuccessful business situation.

Everything stems from communication. You can't do anything without it.

Yet there is a simple way to minimise the impact of this and to create some great habits in your organisation. This can easily be done by using the Takeaway Model.

When you think about the routine of placing your takeaway order, it goes something like this:

"Hello, can I place an order please?" you ask.

"Yes, certainly. What would you like?" they reply.

"Number 11, number 24, two lots of number 32 and a 46," you reel off.

This is the important bit, because they don't say, "Thanks very much it will be ready in 15 minutes. How would you like to pay?"

They do say, "OK, so you'd like one number 11, two number 32 and one number 46, is that correct?"

And here's the BIG LESSON! **They check and clarify before they do anything else**. They do this because they can't afford to make a mistake. They value your order and they want to please you, so that you keep coming back.

It is surprising how many leaders do not use this communication technique when working with their teams.

You have something important to tell someone, which will move your organisation forward towards its objectives. The stakes are high. The value is huge. The time is short.

You pass on the details and move on.

Then you come back with an expectation that things will happen how you expected them to.

They don't always. It's frustrating, time consuming and costly.

The costs are mostly obvious, but there are also many hidden elements.

If your staff let you down they usually will feel awful. This will impact on their productivity. That costs you money, *and* they feel bad.

If only you could adopt the Takeaway Model when giving information to your staff!

How great would it be if you built a listening culture? What if you could create an atmosphere where you **check and clarify** so that everyone is 100% clear?

Of course you don't want to give your staff the impression that they don't listen and they are not clever enough to know what you mean when you are telling them something important, **but when have you ever really stopped to check that what you think in your head is what actually comes out of your mouth AND what has been said has been interpreted in the right way?**

If I say "helicopter", I have a clear image in my head and I know what I'm thinking.

However, what have you got in your head as you read this right now?

I can't see what you're thinking. You can't see what I'm thinking.

But it is so easy to assume we both are thinking the same thing. It's quite unusual to meet someone who takes the time to check and clarify.

What I am not advocating is that you say: "Right, what did I just tell you?!"

I have worked with many very successful leaders who have improved outcomes in their organisations simply by taking time to embed 'check and clarify' into their business culture.

There are two wonderful side effects which come from adopting the Takeaway Model.

Firstly, when people know you will ask them to feedback what you have said, they will take even more care to listen properly.

Secondly, they will tell you what you said and that might not be what you meant (!), so you get better at making what is in your head come out of your mouth!

To do this you have to declare that you are working on YOUR communication skills and you are checking that WHAT YOU SAY IS

CLEAR (not that you are doubting them).

As a truly great leader, it always starts with you. It is you who needs to model excellent communication.

"I'm going to ask you to feedback what you have understood from what I've said, so I can be sure I am being an excellent communicator."

So, next time you have something important to talk to your team about, build in the check and clarify Takeaway Model, just like the people do when you order a takeaway!

This big bit of leadership improvement is free and will save you time, money and gain you respect if you deliver it properly.

8. What is a 1:1 review for?

Over the years I have identified a common barrier in organisations to getting great results.

The barrier nearly always shows up as an area for development in the way that leaders and managers carry out a review of the performance of the people in their teams.

A 1:1 review system is a formal feedback opportunity to provide two-way communication between you and a person in your team.

A 1:1 review is a ***meeting.*** Meetings are also ***a record*** of the fact that your staff's performance is monitored.

The purpose of a review is to discuss a person's performance against the previous targets and standards and to set new targets. The discussion is recorded and agreement is reached about what is recorded and targets set.

This is a huge part of being a manager and is part of the *performance management process,* which is designed to move the company forward towards its goals.

Everything that every person does in an organisation should directly, or indirectly, move the company towards the goals that have been set for the company.

What a 1:1 is NOT:

It is NOT an opportunity to save up any irritating moans about someone's performance and to discuss their poor performance all in one go!

It is not a 'chat'. It is a process.

I think managers should be banned from saying, "Can we have a chat about…?"

Usually the process starts with setting goals/objectives with an employee, which will be linked to the job description and the company plan. The idea is that when the objectives are achieved the company will be successful in reaching its bigger goals and the person will be happy in their work, due to the shared experience of the success of the company and the future job security this brings.

The process is supported by a record of the event.

The point of the record is to ensure that both you and your team member prepare properly for the 1:1 review. An effective review system is a huge benefit to an organisation (if it is effective! It is NOT a paperwork exercise of filling in a form).

It is a dialogue with an outcome that makes a difference to the performance of the member of staff and the manager. (It is two-way communication.)

The record is important, because it helps to structure the discussion and is a way to compare your view of things to your team member's view.

Preparation is key.

Reviewing the performance of an employee (and for the employee to comment on the way they have been managed) needs to be *based on evidence* wherever possible. Evidence is helpful information.

SMART objectives should be set:

S = Specific

M = Measurable

A = Achievable and Agreed

R = Realistic

T = Time bound

But you can add two extras to make it SMARTER (the extra E can be for ethical/exciting and the extra R can be for recorded/reveal and rewarded – but that's up to the organisation).

Important points:

- Plan the process to fall at a time when it is possible to allocate time properly. It is time consuming.

- Preparation is the key.

- Wherever possible there should be agreement on the evaluation of a person's performance. This relies on great questioning skills and use of evidence. It is about a person's performance, not the person.

- The discussion should take place where no one else can hear what is being said.

- Think about the company plan and link objectives to the plan.

- In an area of performance that needs to improve, the actions to improve must be agreed and owned by the employee wherever possible. They should be encouraged to suggest their own action plan with guidance and support.

- A good review will identify any issues that the manager needs to address as well as any the employee needs to address. *It is a two-way process.*

- Listen actively and record accurately.

- Set the next review period during the meeting.

- Agree the record of the meeting and then ask the person to sign the record and date it.

- Treat a review of good performance as carefully as that of performance that is less than expected. Great feedback about great performance is key in a person's development. It needs to be specific, set in context and based on evidence.

Making a mistake in managing someone's performance can have very serious consequences. These can be financial and could even lead you to a court case.

Remember that a 1:1 review done badly can damage a good working relationship, ruin trust, cause resentment and adversely affect the motivation and productivity of a trusted employee.

On the other hand, a great 1:1 review can be highly motivational, improve relationships, create trust and improve productivity.

9. What's the link between success, happiness and performance?

Great leaders create a drive for excellence by using the link between success and happiness. Do you?

My favourite TED talk features Shawn Achor explaining the link between success, happiness and improved performance. This is 12 minutes of pure gold, and well worth a watch.

It's really funny, too. TED Talks are great for personal development. If you've not watched any just search TED Talks and you will disappear down a vortex of short, inspirational videos.

His talk is based on his book, *The Happiness Advantage*, 2010.

This has been profoundly effective for showing clients the importance of a positive attitude when improving performance. Leaders mainly do their best work (and most challenging work) when things need to change for the better.

The powerful learning described by Achor emphasises the findings from research on the brain and within organisations in 44 countries that **a positive brain performs better**. The positivity releases dopamine, which switches on all the learning centres in the brain. This is well worth remembering!

As Achor speaks so quickly you might like to be reminded of a few key points from his film:

- The lens through which you see the world shapes your destiny.

- Your external world can only predict 10% of your long-term happiness (e.g. education, environment, upbringing).

- 90% of your long-term happiness is down to **the way your**

brain processes information.

- Key indicators of happiness and success are your levels of **optimism, your social support and how well you face stress as a challenge.**

- His research has provided a formula to help people in education and industry to train their brains to be positive in the present, so they are more productive, produce better results and achieve more success.

- Focusing the brain to be positive in the present is a habit which can be learnt and practised.

- Doing this has proven to impact significantly on results.

Here's the formula to train the brain to be positive:

1. Focus *each day* on three new things you are grateful for.

2. *Write about a positive experience each day* that has occurred in the last 24 hours – it's important to write about it (journalling).

3. **Exercise helps the brain – do some!**

4. **Meditation –** some moments of stillness help the brain process more effectively.

5. **Conscious or random acts of kindness,** e.g. thanking someone, praising someone, saying/doing nice things.

A habit is something that forms if you do it for two minutes a day for 21 days in a row. Achor has evidence that this formula has transformed business organisations dramatically.

So, here's something significant. How can you use this in your leadership approach?

I have always started any work I do with clients with a review of what has gone well. I had not fully appreciated why this was so helpful, but I can see that having a positive focus has always been very beneficial and helped clients really get into their learning.

I know now that this is a chemical reaction in the brain which has helped the learning go well. I have started to share this Shawn Achor video with clients to explain the significance of this positive start to sessions.

In your leadership role, if you want someone to learn something then you need to achieve a positive focus to start with. *Simple, but helpful*. This links very closely to the skills of providing effective feedback. Many clients I've worked with said they struggled with providing feedback to staff when performance has dropped. Knowing that starting with a positive focus could be the key to helping the individual learn to improve.

10. What leaders need to know about highly exceptional performance. How do highly successful people evolve to be the way they are?

One of the people who has inspired me recently is Robin Sharma. I love his videos and his philosophy. He is famous for his excellent book *The Leader Without a Title*. He works with top CEOs, billionaires and high performers.

I watched his recent video and it moved me so much I read the book. I also gave a copy to all the people in the group I was coaching at the time.

I hope you can see something in it that helps you. The key messages from it are here for you, but I would like to suggest that it is a great way to spend a few minutes. So many things are out there to distract us and to inform us as the hi-tech world of accessible information grows and multiplies!

It is a challenge to be discerning. I sometimes feel I suffer from FOMO (fear of missing out) whilst juggling with information overload! The skill of discernment is a good one to build up to a high level to be able to focus in on what is flashing up in front of us at any one time – what to notice and what to disregard.

The Sharma video is called The Super Producers Secrets – great title! Here's what it says in a nutshell:

- World class performance is a combination of inspiration and execution.
- The execution is what separates exceptional achievers from average ones.
- Execution is developed by mastering three aspects of performance: the philosophy, the psychology and the practise.
- World class performers develop world class habits, rituals and routines.
- There are 24 hours in everyone's days, but high performers use theirs more wisely.
- Based on Anders Ericsson's research (University of Florida) it takes 10,000 hours to become an exceptional master of a craft.
- This 10,000 is spent *installing* habits, rituals and routines, so that performance becomes easy.
- It's not just about talent, genius or flair. It's about choices.

- The work done installing these three elements of how to choose to behave are built in three steps:

  1. The struggle and *war* of changing after deciding.

  2. The *dismantling* of old behaviours.

  3. *Automaticity.*

- *It's not just about a mindset, which you read a lot about.*

- It's the *behaving* that makes the difference.

Here's the bit I loved the most: it's easier to *behave* your way into a new way of thinking than to *think* your way into a new way of *behaving*. *It links nicely back to our earlier chapter on values and behaviours.*

It's about practising. Anders, and thus Sharma, says it takes 66 days to make a habit into **automaticity.**

He says that we should start this today.

He goes on to explain this in the video and in his books:

- He advocates a 20/20/20 system. This involves the first 20 minutes of your day getting sweaty in exercise, followed by another 20 minutes of journalling, re-writing your goals and activating that part of the brain which will help you notice the key opportunities: the reticular activator. Finally, 20 minutes of gratitude.

- He also emphasises that learning is a game changer. Be ready to learn. Make time to learn. (When was the last time you did some personal development?)

- Then he explains the need to focus on the Daily Five, your five important outcomes you desire from each day that will help you move forward.

- He also dwells on the need to exhibit acts of kindness to

build self-esteem and to live a worthy life.

It is interesting that both Achor and Sharma mention kindness.

It connects beautifully with what Mary Portas said about The Kindness Economy.

In addition to this, Dr John Blakey's work outlines nine leadership habits which build trust and the ninth one is 'Choosing to be Kind'.

There is a theme here.

The future success of this planet actually depends on the impact of kindness going forward.

11. What has cottage cheese got to do with your leadership?

If you can answer that question I will be impressed! If you can't, then make sure you read on.

If you do know the answer it probably means that, like me, you are a fan of the great book by another one of my all-time gurus/heroes, Jim Collins. His famous books are renowned for being the go to references when leading an organisation from where it is, to where you really want it to be. His books are on the must read list if you are serious about making an impact and achieving excellent results.

(I am fully aware that I have recommended quite a few books. Just cancel everything for the next few months and read!)

My favourite book of his – the one I encourage all my clients to get to grips with and apply the learning from – is *Good to Great*. It's a truly helpful guide to what it takes to transform your business to the higher limits of success.

There are six key elements to the core principle of the Flywheel

Model, which is a central concept in this great piece of work. The Flywheel Effect was used by Collins to state the fact that companies don't become exceptional as a result of a single intervention or initiative, but rather from the accumulation of little wins that stack up over years of hard work. I'm not going to go into the whole book now, but I do want to draw your attention to the key nugget I alluded to in the heading.

"What's cottage cheese got to do with it?" I hear you cry!

Well, it's quite simple, really. Collins tells the story of the impact of leadership and the matter of those disciplined people who make an organisation great.

This is not 'discipline' as you might think of it. More of a way of living which is built around *habits, rituals and routines* that *drive excellence*.

Are you beginning to get the idea that the books I recommend all have common themes?

Collins explains that the business is driven by excellent systems, which in turn are driven by the right kind of **disciplined people**, who **think** in the right kind of disciplined way and **behave** in the right disciplined way (i.e. take disciplined action).

(We are back to behaviour again!)

One character Collins skilfully uses to illustrate the point of a disciplined approach is Dave Scott. Dave is a *six times* Hawaii triathlon champion. That's no mean feat. *Every day* Dave cycles 75 miles, swims 20,000 meters and runs 17 miles. He is fit.

He is serious about his craft. He practises it. A lot. He has no need really to watch his weight! That amount of activity will burn calories, no trouble.

However, Dave pays attention to detail and is disciplined. ***He makes sure to rinse his cottage cheese to eliminate the excess fat.*** It's the discipline of the habits, rituals and routines that he lives by. It's harder for him to NOT be a master of his craft than it is for him to be it.

There is an important lesson here for all leaders who desire outstanding results. The clue is in the attention to living by the habits, rituals and routines. It's not by chance that Dave can achieve consistently good results in a hugely demanding activity, because he doesn't leave it to chance. Neither should leaders. We can all benefit from constantly improving the odds by working at those incremental subtleties that make the difference.

Here's one: what about how you greet your team? How much attention to detail do you pay to the achievers and the not so good achievers? Do you swoop in like a seagull when things aren't good, but fail to notice when great work is produced?

Or do you avoid paying attention to the detail of poor performance and hope it goes away? You know you need to relentlessly ensure the quality of work is at the right standard, but when it's not, what do you do about it?

Next time you see some cottage cheese think of Dave and then think of your own disciplined approach.

Exercise:

From this section of snippets choose three to deeply embed in your leadership practise and monitor the impact over a period of weeks.

Share your choice openly with your team and challenge them to join you in three significant changes.

CHAPTER TWENTY-SIX

THE FUNDAMENTAL COACHING TOOL – USING THE GROW MODEL

In 2011, I signed up with The Coaching Academy to work towards my Small Business Coaching Diploma. It was life changing for me and truly opened my eyes to leadership and coaching skills. One of the most significant things I learnt was about the GROW Model. This excellent part of any coach's toolkit has been given to us by the outstanding expert in his field, Sir John Whitmore, the author *of Coaching For Performance*, which I mentioned earlier on.

Here is what I learnt.

The GROW Model is a tool.

You can use it to guide someone towards something.

Here's a helpful summary:

G = <u>Goal</u>: What is it specifically that you want to achieve? (Is it a 'be' or a 'do' or a 'have' goal?)

Remember the SMART way to set goals (Specific, Measurable, Realistic/Results-based Agreed, and Time bound).

When will you know you have achieved it? What will success look like?

In which of those areas is it most important to you to make progress, first/now? Focusing on this specific area – on a scale of 1–10 – where are you now? How will you know when you are one step closer to the 10? When can you achieve this by? What would be a good outcome for you for this session?

What would you therefore need to take away from the next X minutes?

R = <u>Reality</u>: Where are you now with this?

Reality questions are there to inspire the client to think and explore:

- The current situation
- Obstacles
- Past experiences
- Who else is involved
- Strengths
- Skills
- Resources

Revisit the facts. Eliminate the possibility of assumptions

- What is happening now?
- What have you done so far?
- What hasn't happened for you?
- What obstacles are you facing?
- What has stopped you doing more?
- What is your main concern?

- Tell me about a time when you were successful in a similar situation?
- What worked well?
- What made the difference?
- What didn't go well?
- What did you learn from that experience?
- What strengths do you have to assist you?
- What inner resource do you need to tap into?
- What skills have you used in the past?
- What strengths would your boss say you have?

Resources: Reminding and opening up choices

- What resources do you have to help you succeed?
- What extra resources will you need?
- What internal resources can you access to assist you?

O = <u>Options</u>: What can you do?

In a safely imagined future what options are there?

List them all, don't judge anything at this stage. Use your creativity to really explore this bit:

- What would your hero do?
- What would the most amazing company in the world do?
- If you had the answer, what would it look like?
- What's the first simple step forward for you?
- What if…?
- What else?

- What is the tried and tested way to overcome this?

- What can you learn from others who have overcome this?

- What would really motivate you?

- What's missing?

Rank the suggestions and evaluate their merits: usefulness, quickest, easiest, impact versus effort, result. How will it look and feel?

W = Way forward/ What will you action? By When?

Write down the commitments you will make to make your goal happen. Be specific and clear. Break down the steps to discover and define the clear action steps to achieve the goal.

HOW will you achieve these actions? Identify three actions.

- What is it about these actions that appeals?

- How realistic is it for you to complete them?

- What impact will they have?

- What will happen if you do not take action?

- Specifically, when will you do that?

- How do you usually remember to do things at the times you want to?

- How will you remember to do it, at this time?

- How realistic are the timeframes?

On a scale of 1–10:

- How committed are you to taking the action?

- How enthusiastic are you about making this happen?

- How challenging is completing this task?

- What would stop you taking action?

- What are you concerned about in relation to these actions?

- How might 'you' get in the way of completing these actions?

- How will taking these actions move you closer to your goal?

- Remind me how you will benefit.

- How will your taking action here impact on others?

- Ultimately, what will taking these actions help you move towards achieving?

- What will help you maintain your motivation?

- What have you learnt from this session?

What I wouldn't advise is to drill your team member with all of these questions in this exact order using it like a checklist, expecting them to answer each one and everyone straight away!

My point is that over time you can structure your work as a leader to build up a repertoire of questions and use your experience to gain insights into what works best in each situation with a particular person. I studied and practised coaching for a long time before it became easier and more effective. My first attempt was like an episode of the BBC1 favourite quiz show Mastermind. The poor guinea pig (my colleague at work) was totally overwhelmed and never volunteered again to be part of my coaching portfolio!

I'm offering this up to you, to help you begin using questions to ask your team what they can do, what they already know and what they might need to do next.

Developing a coaching culture in your organisation might well need an external catalyst.

If you are used to constantly telling people what to do (in one organisation I work with they called this 'barking order') and then you suddenly change over to asking people things, they will wonder what on earth is happening. They will feel insecure and wonder what has happened to you!

You might well need to be coached to become a coach. (If you are looking for a coach to do that, I do know someone…)

However, I can highly recommend beginning a change programme to move towards this approach. I have seen with my own eyes the dramatic effect it can have on the organisation, the results, staff satisfaction levels and the sense of personal achievement felt by those being coached. These effects are all positive and well worth the investment of time, money and effort. It's not a quick fix, but it is a long-term culture change – the gift which keeps on giving!

I'll throw in my favourite quote again here to remind of why this is so great:

> "A leader is best when people barely know he exists. When the work is done, they will say 'We did it ourselves'."
> **— Lao Tzu**

The benefits include:

- Developing highly motivated autonomous learners.
- 'We' overrides 'I'.

- Engagement levels increase.

- Staff sickness goes down.

- Productivity increases.

- Quality improves.

- Speed of execution improves.

- Communication improves.

- People enjoy their work with a sense of pride and ownership.

- Trust prevails.

- People notice improved working relationships.

Plus, when you aren't there people get on with what they are inspired to work towards.

The GROW Model has stood the test of time since coaching emerged in the 1980s.

Bringing this helpful tool into your kit adds a framework to structure your conversations, and I have helped many leaders adapt their style to incorporate it and they have never looked back.

Why not give it a go if you haven't used it before?

Top Tip:

You do not have to use this tool by saying, "Right, now we are going to use the GROW Model!"

You can hold this structure in your mind and work through the steps as you feel it is best.

CHAPTER TWENTY-SEVEN

'SKILL' VERSUS 'WILL' – UNDERSTANDING A
LACK OF WILL

High Skill/ Low Will	High Skill/ High Will
Hobbyists/ Cruisers/ Cherry pickers	High performers and Highly willing
Low Skill/ Low Will	**Low Skill/ High Will**
Non-performers	New staff /Graduates/ Promoted/ Maternity-leavers/ Long-term illness/ New role

I discovered this matrix during a workshop at the Entrepreneurs Circle. It really helped me understand the options available when coaching a person who hasn't engaged fully at work.

The Situational Leadership Model, introduced in the 1970s by Paul Hershey and Ken Blanchard, is explained more fully in the next chapter.

This matrix is part of that model. It unlocked some clarity for me. There is no 'one size fits all' way to manage and coach someone.

When people speak about nature, they often say *"only the fittest survive"*. In my view, that's not the whole story.

The most successful species are the ones which adapt the most effectively to the circumstances in which they find themselves. The ability to adapt is what humans are famous for.

However not all leaders seem to be able to manage it!

Look at what happened during the COVID-19 pandemic. All those restaurants which turned on a sixpence to offer takeaways or deliveries came through it, because they adapted. Those businesses which saw the pandemic as an opportunity, instead of a threat, thrived. Some businesses closed. It's not as clear cut as that, but it is something to think about.

Nigel Botterill is the MD of the Entrepreneurs Circle and he tells a story of a hotel owner he was working with. She had a lovely, little, independent hotel. She was a bit of a 'technophobe'. As the Internet came online, he asked her about her plans to adapt her marketing to include the Internet.

He asked, "What's your strategy for online marketing?"

She replied, "I'm hoping that the Internet goes away."

I don't think she was an adapter.

Hope is not a strategy. (I heard that on a podcast somewhere, but I can't remember where.)

We're in a similar situation with AI (Artificial Intelligence) now – I wonder whether she is still in business and whether she is still hoping.

I challenge leaders to adapt how they interact with people all the time. This means customers and, more significantly, employees.

Adapting to meet the best way the others around you need to be, as best you can, whilst still remaining authentic is the mark of a great leader.

The Skill vs Will Matrix above is just a model, and, of course, there are no actual boxes you put people into. It is just a guide to help you identify what might be going on if someone's work is not at the standard you had *expected*.* It is more that you need to unpick what is actually going on.

Is it because the person doesn't have the skill yet?

Is it because the person is not willing to engage?

(*Note: We will deal with CLEARLY DEFINED EXPECTATIONS a little later. Let's assume you have mastered that part already.)

When using the matrix with clients for whom there is an employee performance issue, I ask the following three questions:

1. When you consider your employees, which boxes would you put individuals in?
2. Which box has the most dangerous combination?
3. What are your responsibilities in response to individuals in each box?

Notes:

- Remember that people do not behave in boxes – it's just a model.
- The activity is much more sophisticated than what is described in those three questions.

- I urge you to consider that all performance issues with employees *start with you as their leader*. It always starts with you.

- The most important person's performance to manage is your own.

Answers to questions 2 and 3 usually cover conversations around the following:

2) A highly willing, poorly skilled employee can cause quite a bit of damage. That's why it is crucial to have a great induction programme, an ongoing staff development programme, excellent review processes, effective communication and highly skilled managers and leaders.

3) If a person is highly skilled, yet unwilling to perform well, how will you know that? What will you be seeing, hearing, feeling? How will you respond? Your responsibility is to notice things, so that it doesn't get to this point! If it does, are you confident and competent to have the conversation to deal with this? Are you willing to accept feedback about your leadership, your processes and your business, generally? If you listen carefully, are you committed to resolving it, having had the conversation?

There is nothing worse for an employee than to explain what the barriers are, which are preventing them from achieving well and to be heard describing how frustrating that is, only to discover that the person they spoke to is not going to take any action.

That's when they leave.

I am speaking from experience here. You may remember from Part One of this book that I have left several employment situations.

You might be familiar with INSET days in education establishments, you know, the days the schools or colleges are closed for staff development.

I did attend many extremely effective training sessions and learnt a great deal. However, back in the days when I worked at a less effective establishment, I also attended some rubbish sessions which were frankly a very expensive waste of everyone's time.

We were regularly invited to work in groups with flip chart paper and marker pens to discuss and note down answers to questions about how things could be improved. We dutifully provided helpful information about processes, equipment, barriers to our effectiveness and things which were generally easy to resolve.

The Senior leadership team would dutifully gather the flip chart sheets in and collate the information.

We NEVER heard anything back or noticed any changes. There was only so much of that I could bear.

The final straw in this category of things which managers do which are a pointless waste of valuable time (particularly in larger organisations) are staff surveys.

Alongside the INSET workshop at my college was the annual staff 'stress survey', which we were compelled to respond to in a very controlling way.

(Of course it was anonymous!)

I watched exhausted colleagues (with incredibly low morale and levels of stress) dutifully complete and return the survey having poured out their hearts and explained what had been causing them to feel so stressed.

I knew that it was never going to change anything. It was going to tick a box for the impending OFSTED or Investors in People accreditation. I was wise to the tick-box activities which had to be carried out. Others might not have been.

Nothing was done to resolve the stress-causing barriers to effectiveness. Nothing ever changed to improve that. Having been asked to provide the information, my colleagues naively thought that steps would be taken to make things better.

Their hearts sank when they realised the exercise was pointless. It was worse than not having been asked about their stress levels in the first place! (See Chapter 48: The Stockdale Paradox).

Finally, on this matrix, I would ask about the bottom left corner where you might identity some non-performers with low skill and low will.

Some roles do not require much skill. That's OK, provided people are willing.

The discovery I have made throughout my career as an employed person and as a leadership coach is this: when somebody recruits a person who subsequently becomes unwilling and remains unskilled, it appears to be quite a difficult decision/activity to manage the performance of that person.

It is often because of a lack of effective recruitment processes leading to a lack of a review of performance which results in a probation period passing and the tough conversation not happening.

In addition to this is the other matter of some people only want to say nice things to people at work. There is more on this later.

Hopefully you are not reading this feeling a bit embarrassed.

I have worked with several business owners who were unable to face the brutal truth that their recruitment choice was a poor one. The longer it went unacknowledged, the worse the situation became.

I'm not willing to coach people who can't admit they have made a mistake.

Admitting your mistakes as a leader is a key behaviour for building trust.

Exercise:

Do you have anything in your past which was a mistake that needs admitting to?

Can you admit to a mistake which you previously hid from, but needs to be dealt with properly?

What action are you prepared to take to build trust over something you might need to amend?

CHAPTER TWENTY-EIGHT
WHAT'S THE SECRET TO MANAGING DIFFICULT PEOPLE?

Many leaders dread managing difficult people. So, what can you do?

Managing difficult people is a common theme which comes up in my work training and when coaching leaders. The good news is there are usually very few difficult people in an organisation, the trouble is they do tend to take up the majority of your time if you are not careful.

In fact, try this activity now:

Take a piece of A4 paper and draw a line down the middle of it (portrait). At the top left of the page write the name of the person who you *know* adds most value to your organisation – there will be a name that comes straight to you.

Under that name, write the name of the next person who adds great value. Continue to make a list down the page of people, in order of decreasing value added, until you get to those names that you heave a sigh of frustration at and dread the thought of.

Next, top left of the page, write the name of the person who is a real drain on your time. Who is it that sucks you dry of time and you just can't bear it? Carry on with this list in order of decreasing time spent with them and decreasing dread factor.

What do you notice about the two lists? Are they inversely proportional?

In most organisations, this is what they find. As a teacher in a classroom, 95% of my time was absorbed with the one or two naughty, distracted pupils who were off task and they took all my focus and energy.

What should you do about this? What makes most sense? To dwell on non-performers, or to dwell where the value is added?

The non-performers need to be managed effectively. Here is a quick guide from Ken Blanchard's *Leadership and the One Minute Manager* series.

In a nutshell people fall into categories based on their competence levels and their commitment levels. How good their commitment and competence levels are can be described as their development (D) level. There are four development levels. For each development level there is an appropriate style of leadership (S).

Here's the breakdown:

D1 = low competence and high commitment which requires a Directing Style (S1) of leadership (lots of structure, organisation, teaching and supervision).

D2 = some/low competence and low commitment which requires a Coaching Style (S2) of leadership (directing, supporting, asking questions, providing feedback, raising awareness and responsibility).

D3 = moderate to high competence and variable commitment requires a Supporting Style (S3) (lots of praise, effective listening and facilitation).

D4 = high competence and high commitment requires a Delegating Style (D4) (handing over responsibility for day-to-day decision-making, checking in and recognising results).

In a busy organisation (and especially when staff turnover is high), leaders sometimes forget to move through this layered system of leadership styles and opt for the one which suits them best.

Or they make assumptions about either competence or commitment. Have you checked with your difficult members of staff whether it is in fact a competence issue and not a commitment issue? If you have a difficult member of staff, have you ever tried a different approach? Have you ever examined what could be different about you?

Very often we see in others what we need to learn about in ourselves.

Of course I'm not saying that there are no awkward sods out there, who are hell-bent on making their boss's life hell! However, these people are few and far between.

Often what is needed with a difficult member of staff is a different approach. Once a competency issue is dealt with (either through training or investigation), then explore the commitment issue.

There are a range of styles available and without having skills in that full range, it is easy to plump for what you know and what works with most people. A one size fits all approach won't always cut the mustard.

Having a range to select from, so the best style is used to identify the best approach for the best result, is more professional and is often what makes an outstanding leader. They have what it takes to mould their approach to meet the needs of the person with whom they are dealing at the time. High skill levels don't grow on trees; they are honed and mastered with experience and development.

The species that adapts the most is most likely to survive.

Exercise:

Take time to do the activity above.

Ask a trusted colleague in your senior team to do the same activity.

Compare results.

Then take the necessary action.

CHAPTER TWENTY-NINE
A GOOD CONVERSATION ABOUT PERFORMANCE

The single biggest struggle I have observed is when a leader or manager finds it a challenge to provide feedback to a person to help them improve what they are doing.

I have seen a frustrated manager walk away from a situation having said nothing to the person to whom they need to deliver this kind of guidance, head straight into another department and explain clearly what is going wrong and what the impact is for themselves, the business, their reputation, the budget and so on. They wax lyrical to anyone else prepared to listen. They hold their head in their hands and moan on about how frustrating it is.

The issue is that they are having a monologue with the wrong person instead of upskilling themselves on how to provide feedback.

They are not taking responsibility for their own part in it. They are happy to moan and remain frustrated. They would rather do that than hold a more challenging conversation.

I need to highlight here that I have a rule around this, which I feel must be set out in every organisation in which I am coaching the leadership and management.

In a transformational leadership approach, feedback is key. It's all about the feedback!

I encourage all leaders and managers to write the following on a sticky note and put it on the computer screen or wherever it is most likely to be viewed.

If you have feedback to provide to a member of the team, you must have been trained first. You must also be willing to receive feedback, however poorly that feedback is delivered to you. There is always learning in feedback however much it hurts a leader. To provide it, you must be willing to receive it.

Here's the way I coach people about providing feedback for improved performance:

- Gather the evidence you have regarding performance which is below what is required.
- Prepare evidence of what the required clearly defined performance standard is (i.e. what good looks like).
- Ask the person to prepare to discuss how they think their work is going at the moment.
- Meet in private and conduct the review along these lines as a guide:
  - "Thanks for preparing for this important meeting. Please tell me about how your work is going from your perspective."
  - Let them talk and listen with your eyes, ears and heart.
  - Ask them why they think their work is going that way and what **evidence** they are using to support their

judgement.

o Explain that you would like to compare this to your perspective on how things are going at the moment.

o "This is the clearly defined standard we have for this role at this time. The evidence from my perspective is that your work is at this level…"

o Demonstrate using a graph as below:

PERFORMANCE

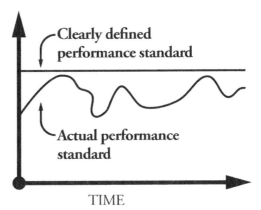

The feedback will be a discussion to elicit how the employee will make changes to improve performance

Clearly defined performance standard

Actual performance standard

TIME

Then go on to ask:

o "Comparing our sets of evidence it is clear that there is a need for the standard of the work to improve, would you agree?"

o Let them talk about this and listen.

• Ask

o "What is the barrier preventing you from reaching this standard at the moment?"

o   Listen with your ears, eyes and heart.

o   Take notes.

o   Identify any areas for support.

o   Then explain the importance of the need to change – the context, the impact, the vision, the team, the results, the customers, the reup.

o   "What specifically would you need to improve your performance?"

o   Listen. Take notes.

o   "What is it that you can change straight away?"

o   Listen. Take notes.

o   "How committed are you to make that change? On a scale of 1 to 10 with 10 being extremely committed and 1 being not likely to change anything, how would you grade your commitment?"

o   If it's not a 10, ask, "What would a 10/10 for commitment to improve look like?"

• Always ask "What else?" because there nearly always is something else!

o   Make notes of what they say, then ask, "What is preventing you from making a commitment like this a 10/10?"

o   Listen and make notes, then decide whether you need to make any adjustments.

o   Then say, whilst nodding, "So you have agreed to commit to these specific actions… (list them and write them down).

- o Nod and smile and then say, "That's excellent. With these improvements you will be making a great contribution. We will look to review this in (specified time period, make an appointment to meet again). Thank you."

- o "Without the improvement there is a lot at stake. The impact of not improving is serious because (list the impact on the team, results, customers etc.) so thank you for your commitment to improve. I have to highlight there does need to be this consistent level of performance for the company to be secure in the future, which is why we take performance very seriously. When we meet again on (date) I look forward to celebrating the improvement. Failure to improve will result in further investigations and the possibility of consequences for you in your role."

- o "Your objectives are to work specifically on:

  1)

  2)

  3)

- o By (appointment date), when we will meet again to review your success."

- Make notes and send a copy to the person with a copy for HR.

It is the most important skill you can practise if you want performance to improve.

I've made a handy checklist to help you improve the culture of feedback in your organisation.

Feedback checklist

1	I have set a regular diary schedule for 1:1s with my team members and I avoid cancelling these meetings as far as possible. I have explained to all team members the importance of 1:1 reviews with them.	
2	I have a clear plan for my team members and know what they need to achieve in accordance with the company vision and values.	
3	I have the right information about the performance of my team members and share this with them regularly.	
4	I praise and redirect regularly.	
5	I plan properly for my 1:1 reviews with my team and this planning is in my diary/calendar.	
6	I give my team members time to reflect and plan for their 1:1s.	
7	**I store a record of the 1:1 meetings I have with all my team members and provide a copy of these notes to my team members. I refer to the last**	

	review's meeting notes at the beginning of each 1:1 review. I challenge and inspire, praise and redirect.	
8	I arrange for the correct place for my 1:1s – wherever possible the monthly 1:1s take place in a quiet space in private with focus.	
9	I take action to provide feedback in the appropriate time frame.	
10	I make sure that the right person is providing feedback. I take my responsibility for providing feedback seriously.	
11	I strive to be an excellent feedback provider.	
12	I use questions in my 1:1 reviews so that the person takes responsibility for their performance improvement.	
13	I check and clarify that my team members understand their actions from the 1:1 review.	
14	I ask my team members how I can improve to help them improve in all my 1:1s.	
15	I feed back about improvements that can be made at every opportunity to all staff and I do this as an expert so that they welcome the feedback.	

16	In the 1:1 review, the team member talks for 80% and I talk for 20% of the time.	
17	The 1:1 creates an opportunity for SMART targets wherever possible and appropriate.	
18	I am willing to receive feedback about my performance because I value learning to improve, even if the person providing feedback to me is not yet an expert.	

Getting it wrong – a common mistake

I have observed the following common mistake.

In my 30+ years of studying leadership and management, there have been some excellent examples of classic mistakes you must avoid. In all the different organisations in which I have been either employed or I have worked with as a leadership coach there are a few themes which stand out as really dreadful examples of leadership. The great news is that these are things from we can all learn from and work on, to avoid making them, too.

One of my best friends is a dedicated professional, who strives for excellence in whatever role she performs. I've never been surprised to hear about her successful promotions over the years and always thought how lucky each company who has had the pleasure of employing her has been.

She told me something which highlights a classic, tragic mistake her employer made.

My friend fulfilled the role of Department Manager in every way except in actual title and pay, whilst a huge hole in staff cover was left to fester, without any action to replace the missing person.

In essence, my friend worked over and above the required standard and took on many responsibilities, so the department achieved its objectives. She did this because she cared passionately about the organisation and what it stood for – and because she was capable of doing so.

Occasionally someone more senior had popped in and said, "Well done," but nobody had actually noticed *specifically* the massive impact her work had and what the consequences of her not doing it would have been.

The senior team had lost touch with what that department did on a daily and monthly basis. They had also become accustomed to my friend's high standards and outstanding attitude and taken her for granted.

All of that would not be so terrible if it weren't for the final blow. When her review came, she mentioned the extra work she had been doing and provided evidence of how well she had managed the department, with real data and results to prove her impact.

The senior team then took that data and celebrated the results as their own and failed to recognise my friend's success. In addition to that they offered her a year's temporary contract as Acting Manager (as the absent staff member wasn't coming back).

Wait for it… they offered her £100 per year extra! Yes, that's right, £100 per year, which is about £2 per week. That's how much they valued her extra work, the sacrifice she made in her personal life, the care and attention to detail and the excellent attitude towards the organisation. She said, "It felt like a kick in the teeth."

The organisation did not need to find a replacement, because my friend had somehow managed to squeeze all the extra work in around her own, but not without its detrimental effects to her. My friend did not leave work until everything had been completed and nothing had been left that would negatively affect the organisation.

It is remarkable that something as obviously wrong as this can happen.

On so many levels the senior team had been reckless. They failed to notice the impact of a missing member of management, failed to notice the excellent member of staff saving them masses of headaches and inconvenience of finding a replacement, failed to properly acknowledge the outstanding work of an employee, failed to value her attitude and commitment, failed to recognise and share her example, effort, commitment, had taken the credit for her hard work and – worst of all – thrown a token gesture of value, which was tantamount to rubbing salt in the wound.

What is so sad here is that this is not an isolated case. I have heard this story in organisations over and over again.

There's loads to learn, though, not just for the senior team in that particular organisation. My friend needed to be a better communicator and to clarify her situation. She was hoping, someday, to be promoted to Department Manager, which would be the logical next step for her. She needed to clarify what was expected of her and what the outcome would be. The senior team needed to learn to pay attention to what was happening under their noses and to act properly to save themselves the trouble of finding two new members of staff.

That's right. Not only will the absent member of staff not be coming back, my friend has left too.

What are the lessons for an excellent leader?

1. Never be too busy to notice what's going on under your nose.
2. Never take an excellent member of staff for granted (it's all too easy to devote all your time to those staff members who are not performing well).
3. Never take credit for work that has been done by someone else.
4. Always recognise excellent work when it is over and above what would normally be expected.
5. Always notice and value a person's commitment and excellent attitude.

Obvious stuff but very often it's the obvious things that get overlooked.

If it's obvious, **be curious**.

Providing positive feedback is also a specific skill in the same way that having a good conversation about performance that is not at the required standard.

I don't know whether you are old enough to remember the BBC sitcom *Are You Being Served?*

The show was about a department store (a bit like House of Fraser or Army and Navy).

The action was based around the clothing area where the menswear and ladieswear were across the floor from each other.

Captain Peacock was the Floor Manager. His boss was Mr Granger, Head of the Store, and above him was Young Mr Grace.

Mr Grace was a very frail, old man who resided on the top floor. He could hardly walk, so used two walking sticks to keep him upright. He stole the show in his rare appearances, in which he would descend from the top floor via the lift, the doors would open making a very satisfying *woosh* sound and he would creep slowly out. He would raise one of his walking sticks in the air saying, "You've all done very well!"

I am often reminded of this image when I hear people attempt to boost morale with phrases designed to perk people up.

"You're such a star!"

"Good job!"

"Nice work!"

And so on.

If you are going to provide feedback about good work then use the checklist in the previous chapter.

CHAPTER THIRTY

CAN DAVID BECKHAM TEACH YOU ABOUT FAILURE AND LEADERSHIP?

He might be classed by some as a national treasure.

And he features in another of my favourite and significantly helpful leadership books, *Black Box Thinking* by Matthew Syed. Here is a crucial nugget to take your leadership forward from a celebrity figure. Syed describes the importance of failure by telling Beckham's story.

It was 30th June 1998. Beckham was 23. He was playing in his first World Cup, and this was the crucial knockout match against Argentina for a place in the quarter finals. After serious provocation from Diego Simeone, Beckham lashed out and England's rising star was sent off in front of 20 million fans watching the game.

England lost the game and Beckham became the most hated man in England.

He needed security guards afterwards. He received bullets in the post. Many pundits said it could end his career. How could he come back from that?

But they didn't know the whole story about Beckham and his relationship with failure.

Leadership and great achievers must learn to love failure.

SPEND TIME WITH ME

Let me explain.

Beckham was six when he started to learn about failure and what it taught him. He spent three years practising 'keepy-uppies' to hone his ball control skills. At first, he could manage 50 touches of the ball, aged six. By the age of nine he could manage a record-breaking 2003 touches, without losing control. He practised at every available moment. Beckham knew that each failure was an opportunity to learn. He stuck at it and became a master of that part of his craft.

He then turned his attention and discipline to free kicks. His dad reflects that he must have seen his son take at least 50,000 free kicks in the park. He failed until he got it. He understood failure as the key to improvement.

The next big game straight after Beckham was sent off in 1998, he had to block out the mistake. He had learnt from it. He wanted to improve, and he most definitely bounced back after it. He became quite a good footballer!

Beckham could be said to have a Growth Mindset.

In 2010, Jason Moser, a psychologist at Michigan State University, carried out one of many studies to try to understand the human brain and its response to failure. Using an electroencephalography (EEG) cap and electrodes to measure voltage fluctuations in the brain, Moser wanted to see what was happening at a neural level when mistakes are made.

He investigated two brain signals, one being the Error Related Negativity (ERN) coming from the part of the brain which helps to regulate attention. It's largely involuntary. The other being Error Positivity (Pe) which comes from a different part of the brain and is linked to heightened awareness and comes when we focus on mistakes.

From previous studies, Moser understood that people tend to learn more quickly when their brains show a larger ERN signal and a steady Pe.

To build on this research, he recruited a group of participants, which he organised into two groups. The first group had responded to a questionnaire showing that they tended to have a 'Fixed Mindset' – i.e. they believed things such as "You have a certain amount of intelligence, and you can't really do much about it."

The other group had responded to the questionnaire showing they had a 'Growth Mindset'. They believed you can work on being smart through persistence and dedication.

The questionnaire polarised the respondents and overcame the general view that most people hold, which is that success is based on a combination of talent and practice.

Moser's experiment measured electrical activity in the brain as participants in the two groups carried out tasks and occasionally made mistakes.

The Fixed and Growth Mindset groups provided significantly different results for the Pe reading. Some readings were three times higher. Growth Mindset participants paid much more attention to their mistakes, and this correlated with improved performance.

Getting involved with your mistakes is a great way to improve performance. The results from Moser's experiment discussed in Syed's book are just a small part of the research taking place into the brain and peak performance.

Syed's book tells us in detail about the need to learn from failure. In a nutshell, "When we engage with our errors we improve." (Syed 2016)

Leaders need to take this on board in their organisational culture. There is no learning when blame prevails. People who think about their errors, engage with them, discuss them, own them, can reflect and learn from them to improve their performance. People will not do this if they are afraid to admit mistakes.

A culture of learning can be created when healthy discussion can take place around what goes wrong. Successful companies understand this and embed a learning culture, as opposed to a blame culture. The work of Carole Dweck is outlined in Syed's book around the benefits of a Growth Mindset in a workforce. More honesty and collaboration are generated, which minimises the drawbacks of fear of failure.

Innovation comes from solving problems. Being scared dampens creativity. Creativity and Growth Mindsets are linked. In the modern economy, being able to adapt is key.

There is so much in Syed's book about the need to engage with failure. I would go as far as to say that leaders need to love failure, so they can build a culture of learning from it. This enables improvements to take place at every opportunity.

Beckham is one of many successful people living this way. He might not be the most obvious person to teach you about how to be an excellent leader, but he certainly understands excellence and learning.

Of course, learning from mistakes requires one to be able to admit them first.

Exercise:

Reflect on how willing you are to learn new things.

What happens in your organisation when a person challenges the status quo by recommending improvements to the way things have been done for a long time?

Is the culture one in which suggestions are listened to carefully?

What happens when there is a difference of opinion around how things can improve?

What criteria is used to select new ideas?

CHAPTER THIRTY-ONE
WHY DO SOME LEADERS HATE
DELEGATING?

The trouble is, if it's not done properly delegation does have a bad reputation.

When asked why they hate delegating, people often respond with:

- It's quicker to do it myself.

- Work never gets done the way I like it to be done.

- By the time I've told them how to do it I might as well have done it anyway.

- My team are too busy to give them anything else.

- Getting people to do my work makes me feel lazy.

- I'm not able to trust my team.

These types of comments are indicative of a bigger picture which I'm going to explore.

Getting delegation right is a skill with *long-term benefits*. It is not a sticky plaster fix. It is something to get good at, because the rewards will come back to you further down the line.

Viewing delegation as 'getting rid of something onto someone else' is not delegating. That's dumping on someone. (Covey discusses this in the *Seven Habits of Highly Effective People*.)

The brutal truth is that you can only have a successful and sustainable business if delegating is part of the leadership culture. It does not stand in isolation. It is part of effective leading.

Delegation does sometimes go wrong. For example, here's a true story:

(Adapted from www.businessballs.com)

Maria started work at the toy factory.

She had her induction training day. She was enthusiastic and attentive. Brian was pleased he had got himself a good worker.

Maria listened carefully and returned to work the next day ready to get stuck in and prove herself.

She was working on the "Tickle Me Elmo" production line.

Brian came out of the office to see how she was doing and couldn't believe his eyes.

He was disappointed to see Maria was very behind in her work. It was all piling up around her. She was getting very stressed and looked horrified.

Brian went over to investigate.

He found the problem.

Maria was bent over with a sewing needle and threads, some felt, some scissors and a packet of marbles.

She was carefully cutting small sections of the felt materials, wrapping it around two marbles to cover them and painstakingly sewing them onto Elmo between his legs.

Brain realised he had not been clear enough with his instructions…

"I asked you to give Elmo two 'test tickles'."

How much time is wasted through inadequate delegation?

Why delegate?

If it's viewed so badly and it can go wrong, why are leaders urged to delegate?

Delegation is commonly defined as the shifting of authority and responsibility for particular functions, tasks or decisions from one person (usually a leader or manager) to another. 15 Apr 2019

https://www.smartbrief.com › Originals › Education

The issue is that as a leader you have a value which goes beyond your worth generated by just 'doing stuff'. The value comes from much more than that. A doer has a certain value, but as a person paid to lead the organisation onwards, you need to be able to see clearly and step back from getting too bogged down in day-to-day things.

It's true that you **can do anything**, but equally true **you can't do everything**. (James Allem said that.)

Saying yes to one thing is saying no to something else. *What are you* ***not*** *doing because you are not delegating?*

The art of delegation is to make sure you are doing things that really make the best use of your skills.

Let's look at each of the common moans or pet hates about delegation:

It's quicker to do it myself.

This may be true in the short term, but how many times will you do it yourself? Add those all up and it's not really quicker.

Also, you may be spending your time on something which is at the expense of doing something much more impactful. It's **the**

opportunity cost of what you are not doing that is the hidden cost.

Work never gets done the way I like it to be done.

This comes down to the ability to let go. Not letting go could be holding your company and your career back. It's about learning to risk a little to gain a reward.

It can also be about communicating properly, so that the other person does the work exactly the way you need it to be done. Is it that delegation is the problem, or is it about being too busy or not being an effective enough communicator to explain the work clearly?

By the time I've told them how to do it I might as well have done it anyway.

This could be true, but thinking about the longer term is crucial for a sustainable business. Take this to the extreme and there would never be any staff development. Nothing would change and nobody would grow or develop. It also says to the other people you could delegate to that there is no future. It is a real turn off to have a leader who won't delegate. This can lead to low morale and low productivity, diminishing the other person's value.

The art of good delegation is part of progression planning.

You need to be constantly developing your team for the organisation to be excellent.

My team are too busy to give them anything else.

This could be true, but you need to be sure that you are not assuming this. If there is a chance for someone else to step up to doing something more challenging and stimulating, they may well leap at the chance. It could be that there is no capacity, but be sure of this before making this decision yourself. If you are not careful, you may be guilty of only ever delegating boring routine tasks. That wouldn't be good long term. You want to be a leader who is developing your team, not dumping on them. Teaching your team effective time management is crucial. Role modelling is too.

A key part of the art of delegating is knowing what to delegate and to whom.

Getting people to do my work makes me feel lazy.
This is common as leaders feel proud to be able to cope, especially when they are first promoted to a leadership role. They feel they must prove themselves and be on top of everything.

It might feel like asking someone to take on something from you looks like you are not coping. You really have to think hard about this. All your other leadership skills come into play here. The right mindset to lead and the right communication skills are key. Without these, delegation is much harder.

You really need to know your team and their capabilities and to know about their workload. You also need to feel like a confident leader to get this right. It is about so much more than just 'delegating'.

I'm not able to trust my team.
This is a big issue. You can only gain trust if you give trust. If you don't trust them, they won't trust you. Trust is vital to any organisation. You are only a leader if you have followers. If you want people to follow

you, they need to trust you! So you need to trust them.

Why is it important? Stephen Covey (the world-famous leadership guru who has spent decades studying effective leadership and the impact it has on successful organisations) says this about his research:

"My experience is that significant **distrust doubles the cost of doing business** and **triples the time it takes to get things done.** Trust is like a performance multiplier, enabling organisations to succeed in their communications, interactions, and decisions, and to move with incredible speed. A recent Watson Wyatt study showed that **high trust companies outperform low trust companies by nearly 300%!"**

Therefore, not trusting your team will mean you cannot be an effective leader.

A quick guide to generating trust from Covey's work: *13 Behaviours of High-Trust Leaders Worldwide*

1. Talk straight
2. Demonstrate respect
3. Create transparency
4. Right wrongs
5. Show loyalty
6. Deliver results
7. Get better
8. Confront reality
9. Clarify expectation
10. Practise accountability
11. Listen first
12. Keep commitments
13. Extend trust

Delegation is about balance.

The key is balancing your needs with the needs of the person you are delegating to.

Your needs:

- Time to plan
- WHAT are the task details – what is the OBJECTIVE? These need to be SMART (Specific, Measurable, Agreed and Action based, Realistic and Time bound)
- HOW you want the task done
- How much freedom you are prepared to give
- Information on progress and time scales

The person's needs:

- The chance to discuss the work
- Instructions they can understand
- Support
- The authority to proceed
- Confidence, skills
- Time to ask questions

Delegation is not abdication.

Remember that despite delegating the work to someone else, you remain *accountable*.

Definition – Accountability means having the responsibility and authority to act and fully accept the natural and logical consequences for the results of those actions. You cannot delegate accountability.

There needs to be a culture of accountability for this to work well.

This means there is a climate where people can speak openly, **admit to mistakes without fear**, and worry more about serving the customer (and the team) than saving face.

This starts at the top of the organisation and must be demonstrated most significantly by leaders. You cannot expect others to live this way if the leadership team does not do this themselves.

Great leaders are those who always look to praise their team when things go well (not taking the credit), but when things go wrong, they look to themselves to remain accountable. It all starts with you, the leader.

There are 16 steps to effective delegation:

1. Set time aside to plan and prepare how to delegate effectively. Make notes to share.
2. Discuss and define the decision-making processes. Clarify on authority. Write down what you agree.
3. Agree what the person can decide and when should they defer to you. Record this clearly.
4. Explain why the task needs doing and why you have chosen this person to do it.
5. Find out how they feel about the task. Are they happy to rise to the challenge? Do they have any fears or concerns?
6. Reassure the person over any fears or concerns. Give time and permission to ask questions.
7. Give details about what exactly needs doing by when, including any flexibility. Note this clearly.
8. Set a SMART objective. (Specific, Measurable, Agreed/Action-

based, Realistic, Time bound). Record these details.

9. Agree the next steps and how they would be best achieved. Check how the objective will be broken down. Write this down.

10. Check understanding of the result you are looking to achieve *and how the task fits into the wider picture.*

11. Discuss the significance of the outcome.

12. Agree a timeline for progress reports and agree how monitoring will occur. Record this for reference.

13. Ask if there are any questions.

14. CHECK AND CLARIFY UNDERSTANDING and TIMESCALES (ask person to feedback).

15. Remain accountable.

16. Check in regularly as per the agreement to feedback, redirect and praise.

WRITE NOTES AT EVERY STEP.

Exercise:

Take time out to examine how well you and your management team delegate.

Try the delegation checklist for a period of time and then seek feedback from your employees about whether this approach helps them tackle new or more demanding tasks.

Check that the work you delegate is not just the boring tasks!

Review whether automation or AI can help reduce repetitive tasks out of your processes.

Ask your staff what tasks they think could be automated.

CHAPTER THIRTY-TWO
ACCOUNTABILITY – PLEASE SEND SOMEONE TO BLAME!

"I'm going to hold you accountable." What does that mean to you?

Some people shudder when this is said to them. There can be an element of fear surrounding accountability. I believe this comes from fear of failure.

In many average or poor performing organisations, there is a lack of accountability and a culture of blame. This prevents learning, leading to, at best, average performance. This starts at the top, as do all elements of a culture, and means that someone needs someone else to blame.

My favourite definition comes from the excellent book *Winning With Accountability: The Secret Language Of High-Performing Organizations* by Henry J. Evans. He says:

"Accountability means having the responsibility and authority to act and fully accept the natural and logical consequences for the results of those actions… Clear commitments that – **in the eyes of others** – have been kept."

In excellent or world-class organisations, the high standard is driven by accountability.

Evans' book explains that accountability doesn't stand alone. It forms part of a tripod.

The three legs of the tripod are:

- Responsibility
- Authority
- Accountability

How do you create a balanced tripod?

Firstly, creating accountability demands setting *clear expectations*. There must be a clear understanding of responsibilities (clarity of expectation) set by all leaders.

(I did state that we would get to this. It is a very significant element of successful and effective leadership.)

Secondly, the *authority* necessary to fulfil these responsibilities must be available.

Thirdly, there must be *consequences*.

Evans believes a culture of accountability means that all team members are holding each other accountable for their results and this has very positive effects, including greater accuracy, more vigilant problem-solving, better decision-making, more co-operation and higher satisfaction.

An accountability culture has three main themes:

- Focus
- Influence
- Consequences

The trick, according to Evans, is to develop a climate in which people can speak openly, **admit to mistakes without fear**, and worry more about serving the customer than looking better than a co-worker. Focus, influence and consequences are key.

Focus and influence

Do your teams:

- Clearly communicate and continually reinforce the organisation's mission and vision?
- Establish clear standards of excellence for members?
- Track and analyse their own performance data and use performance feedback as the basis for meetings and problem-solving sessions?
- Analyse work practices for improvement and act?

Consequences

Do you:

- Tie rewards and compensation/pay to team output?
- Allow teams to share in the financial success of the organisation?
- Do what you say and say what you mean, *all the time*?
- Publicly own up to your own mistakes and accept consequences for them?
- When mistakes or problems occur, focus on the future?
- Remember that intent is not the same as performance?
- Help people follow through on their commitments, by regularly checking in on progress?
- Be explicit about accountability and expectations, be supportive and *offer help when they are stuck or unsure*?

In the weakest teams, there is no accountability.

In mediocre teams, bosses are the source of accountability.

In high performance teams, peers manage the vast majority of performance problems with one another.

To build a culture of accountability to ensure results, you must start with yourself and the leaders in your organisation. *You must 'live' accountability.*

You must set out crystal clear expectations. You must model and coach accountability.

"**Ambiguity** is the Achilles' heel of accountability, but **specificity** enables you to **raise the standards** of your team's performance."
— **Lee Colan, Founder of the L Group, co-founder of The L Group, Inc., a Dallas, Texas-based consulting firm that has been equipping and encouraging leaders since 1999. I found his handy quote on this matter online.**

On the subject of accountability, I summarise that going forward it would be beneficial to:

- Set clear expectations
- Tell stories
- Model it
- Coach it.

Set clear expectations.

This single piece of guidance will dramatically improve productivity and results once you have mastered it properly.

There is power in clarity.

Leadership, responsibility and blame – what's the connection?

How well do you understand the significance of 'responsibility' as a leader?

You may be familiar with this story in your organisation:

Whose job was it?

This is a story about four people named Everybody, Somebody, Anybody and Nobody.

There was an important job to be done and Everybody was sure that Somebody would do it, but Nobody did it.

Somebody got angry about that, because it was Everybody's job.

Everybody thought Anybody could do it, but Nobody realised that Everybody wouldn't do it.

It ended up that Everybody blamed Somebody when Nobody did what Anybody could have done.

This is a common story in organisations where leaders need more training. The fact that being a leader is all about taking responsibility is often misunderstood. Some leaders feel that taking responsibility is about doing everything themselves and not delegating much. "I can do it better and more quickly if I do it myself" is often justification I hear when challenging leaders on this. (See Chapter 31.)

The other misunderstanding about responsibility is that some leaders swing into blaming mode and mistake raising awareness of responsibility as ***creating a blame culture.***

Let's start by taking a long look at responsibility. What does it mean?

Here's the dictionary definition again: The state or fact of having a duty to deal with something or of having control over someone.

There is undoubtedly a clear link between success and responsibility.

For example, it is the Flight Captain's responsibility to ensure all the relevant safety checks are carried out correctly before take-off. It is the teacher's responsibility to take an accurate register at the beginning of class. It is the waiter's responsibility to accurately record what the customer chooses from the menu.

Have you ever stopped to check your understanding of responsibility in your leadership role? Have you ever asked your team what it means to them? Have you ever checked that you have a clear understanding throughout your organisation? What does 'taking responsibility' mean to you?

It's a great activity to undertake. Try this:

1. Ask your team to agree a definition of what responsibility means. You may be surprised at how this varies across the team members.

2. Ask the team to each give examples of the type of behaviour that you can see in your organisation which demonstrates a person is ***willing*** to take responsibility. What does it look like? What does it sound like? Where do you see this behaviour? Get them to be very specific.

3. Ask them also to do this for when someone is ***able*** to take responsibility, as above. There may a slight difference. After all,

someone can be willing, but not able and vice versa. (A motivated fool can do a lot of damage!)

4. Hopefully they will provide answers such as being proactive, positive, volunteering, asking questions, looking after other employees' needs (e.g. new staff), learning new skills, asking to learn new skills, finding solutions, feeding back useful information, to name a few.

5. Next, ask them to repeat this activity of identifying a person's behaviours when they are not willing or not able to take responsibility. What does this look like, feel like, sound like?

6. Answers will possibly include: negativity, remaining isolated, hiding information, being reluctant, struggling and not asking for help, moaning, feeling powerless, blaming.

7. Next ask the team to dwell on the consequences of the behaviours of not being willing or able to take responsibility.

In essence, this activity may throw up some useful insights and could teach the team that failing to understand the significance of taking responsibility could cost the organisation dearly.

Ultimately though, nothing is more important for a leader than to role-model this key piece of behaviour. Leadership is about taking personal responsibility for your actions in the first instance, so that you have the credibility to teach others to do the same.

"Success on any major scale requires you to accept responsibility. In the final analysis, the one quality that all successful people have is the ability to take responsibility." **- Michael Korda**

Korda is an English-born writer and novelist who was editor-in-chief of Simon & Schuster in New York City. I came across this quote whilst researching this book.

> "There is a clear link between expertise in leadership and the ability to take responsibility. The more you are willing to accept responsibility for your actions, the more credibility you will have."
> — **Brian Koslow**

Brian Koslow is the founder and president/CEO of Breakthrough Coaching, Inc. a company that provides business training to professionals who aspire to become top earners in their fields.

Remarkable managers are obsessed with accountability. They realise that the success of their direct reports is their success. (If I help you to have success, I help myself to have success). This links nicely to my favourite quote by Lao Tzu at the beginning of Part Two.

On the flipside, they share in failures and mistakes. They hold regular one-to-one meetings with their direct reports and reinforce the outcomes they and the team are responsible for. They are vested in driving solution-based cultures and strive to build an environment of continued learning (versus finger pointing).

Also, to keep staff focused, they make sure to handle and manage accountability conflicts as they come up (instead of letting things fester).

In essence it is about developing trust-based relationships in a coaching culture in which expertly given feedback is part of the normal behaviour.

CHAPTER THIRTY-THREE
HANDLING A POTENTIAL CONFLICT
SUCCESSFULLY

Understanding how to handle conflict was a massive breakthrough for me. I had to work on this because I wanted to help my clients benefit from dealing with conflict more effectively. It was so revealing and helpful.

In order to understand conflict, it is helpful to understand your own levels of assertiveness. (See Chapter 25.)

What is conflict? Have you ever stopped to consider this?

What comes to mind when you hear that word?

- Stress/emotion?
- Defensive behaviours (self and company) if mistakes are made?
- Aggressive behaviours such as voices being raised, less polite language, abrupt tone/stern voice?

Basically, when there is a conflict there is a disagreement, a perceived incompatibility of goals.

What are the components of conflict?

- Disagreement
- Wanting different outcomes

- Aiming for a positive result a 'win/win' – some people!

- Fear of financial loss

- Fear of loss of dignity

- Fear of hurting someone's feelings

- Fear of getting hurt

- Fear of rejection

- Need to establish that both sides in the situation realise that there is a conflict going on.

Often a component of conflict is about shifting blame.

Conflict happens physically, externally and internally.

To sum up, there is a conflict when:

- Both people know there is a disagreement

- There is incompatibility of goals

- There is emotion (mostly not in a good way)

- It is felt that there is fault or blame

- There is a physical internal and external reaction.

There are positives to a conflict which is helpful to remember. In each conflict situation there is an enormous opportunity to learn and grow.

The fact is there will always be times when there is the potential for conflict.

Learning how to cope best in a situation with the potential for conflict is a great skill to have in your tool kit.

It is an opportunity to test that we still hold our values strongly and are prepared to stand up for them.

We need to hold our values high, which means that we need to stand up for them when they are compromised. This is why conflict feels challenging. We must step out of a comfort zone and move into the stretch zone.

Control – yes or no? We can't control how someone will react.

Influence – yes or no? We *can't influence* how someone responds.

Accept/adapt – we do have to accept that conflict is a part of life. We can learn how to cope with it. Can we adapt anything?

The reason it feels bad to be in a conflict situation is most probably down to not wanting to compromise our **values** and not wanting to hurt someone or to be hurt.

	HIGH	X + Y = Z	HIGH
	I'm OK **You're not OK** Win : Lose A.HOLE	**I'm OK** **You're OK** Win : Win RESULT!	
SELF-REPSECT	**I'm OK** **You're not OK** Lose : Lose DISASTER!	**I'm OK** **You're not OK** Lose : Win VICTIM	
	LOW		LOW

LOW   RESPECT FOR OTHERS   HIGH

The four box grid overleaf helps to show the outcomes of a conflict situation when different levels of respect for oneself is compared to the levels of respect for others.

The most ideal outcome is when both parties in a conflict have high levels of awareness of self and others.

(Top right.)

In Stephen Covey's *Seven Habits of Highly Effective People* he dwells on this. In fact, there is a whole chapter on it as it is habit number four.

The only real solution to a conflict is a win:win. If anyone loses, then ultimately everyone loses.

A compromise is just a sticking plaster.

If it is between option A or option B and you go with A, then all those attached to option B have to compromise.

Compromise comes back to bite you in the end.

Compromise gets stored up as resentment. It festers in the background.

It's the same the other way round, if you go with option B, the A people fester.

So, what can you do?

You have to agree on something!

Agree to keep talking!

You all need to work on finding an option C where everyone wins.

Everyone has a conflict pattern

We all have our own one of these and it might not be the best it could be, until we decide to work on it and make it better. It's a great bit of personal development to have achieved, especially if the pattern you have at the moment is not working!

This pattern depends on your:

- Personality
- Culture
- Upbringing
- Education
- Work history

You can't change your past, but you can learn from it and use your experience to guide you towards looking at what is working for you and what is not.

In a conflict situation we may be guilty of attaching to the 'story' of what has happened so far.

As human beings we can edit bits of memory to suit ourselves. We also delete bits, distort bits and embellish bits – it depends on what is at stake. We all do this without realising it. Our perception is our reality, however, there is often more than one way to perceive a situation.

It is important to learn to choose how to feel.

A good technique to learn for managing a conflict situation is made up of stages:

Stage 1: Reaction. Notice how you are reacting (notice how you feel, separate who you are from how you feel, then link back to what it is exactly you are thinking to make you feel this way).

Stage 2: Reflection. Think about how else you can think, what evidence there is – is it reliable? Is it possible to look at this another way?

Stage 3: Response. How do you choose to respond? What is the best combination of being both assertive and co-operative you can offer? How high is your level of respect for yourself and for others?

Stage 4: Attention. What details have been missed, what have you noticed? Notice how you are being. Is it your best self? What can you control? What can you influence? What can you accept?

Stage 5: Venting. Sometimes it is important to allow emotions to vent. This can be you or the other person. Do not become attached to these feelings, or what you hear, but let them air/vent, and look for facts amongst the emotions. Allow space for both sides to vent.

Stage 6: Repetition. Both sides should be aware of repeating old patterns of conflict behaviour. You can only be responsible for your own behaviour, but you might be able to notice someone else's old pattern, if you know them well. Make sure you are not holding on to old conflict patterns, as they might not be helpful.

I learnt about the following coaching framework from Cinnie Noble who is a Conflict Management Coach and Conflict Specialist. Cinnie is the Founder of **CINERGY** Coaching, and she has kindly given me permission to share her model with you. This model is based on conflict management, neuroscience and coaching principles and is specific to interpersonal disputes. That is, these are helpful steps to follow when focusing on a conflict with another person, considering the dynamic and how to move from upset to reset. This is a linear model that requires us to take time and methodical consideration of each stage.

1.   **Clarify your goal.**

In this first stage the question to answer is: what action do we want to take regarding the dispute?

2. **Inquire about the situation**

   In this step it's important to recount what occurred between us and the other person and consider what's most important to you.

3. **Name the elements**

   This stage deconstructs the conflict, requiring close reflection on not only what pattern we followed but also what we noticed about what happened for the other person. This is aimed at developing a sense of mutuality between us. For instance, it's a time to consider what started the conflict for both of us and the assumptions we made about the other, the consequences we are experiencing and other elements that are having an impact on the relationship.

4. **Explore choices**

   In this step we consider what choices we have to reach the goal previously stated (stage 1), now that we have broken down what occurred and given the situation more thought. It's a time to reflect on what might work to achieve that objective considering what is possible for us and what might also work for the other person.

5. **Reconstruct the situation**

   Now there's a plan in place, this is when we figure out how to execute it considering the challenges we might have in doing so. We may, for instance, practise a conversation, or otherwise figure out what strategies will help make our goal a reality.

6. **Ground the challenges**

This step is a time to consider what will get in the way of proceeding with the plan we worked out, having gained clarity on it and how to proceed. Any further challenges we hadn't contemplated and fears or other concerns that may preclude moving forward are addressed here.

7. **Yes to the commitment**

This final stage requires us to be precise on when we are going to carry out our action, committing to the plan we considered.

The full work by Cinnie Noble can be found here:

Noble, Cinnie (2012) *Conflict Management Coaching: The **CINERGY** Model*

https://cinergycoaching.com/conflict-management-coaching-cinergy-model/

Noble, Cinnie (2014) *Conflict Mastery; Questions to Guide You*

https://cinergycoaching.com/conflict-mastery-questions-guide/

The most significant area of conflict is usually within us.

I know you have a big reading list now, but here's another to add to your list:

Getting to Yes with Yourself (& Other Worthy Opponents) by William Ury.

It's a great book for personal discovery and does help with confidence building too.

CHAPTER THIRTY-FOUR
HOW CAN A CARAVAN HELP YOU BE A BETTER LEADER?

Do you ever find you have a day when you don't feel 10/10 or, worse still, you don't feel like a successful leader?

This happens more regularly than you might imagine, even with very successful people.

Getting promoted to a leadership role can suddenly make you feel a bit of self-doubt. You leave a relatively comfortable place, knowing everything and exactly how to get results, then you find yourself managing other people's workloads and it can feel like herding cats! This can make you feel wobbly and despair can set in. (It's very common for this to come flooding in after the initial euphoria of promotion.)

Confidence can vanish remarkably quickly.

The thing is, when this happens, if you have a helpful coping mechanism, you can learn to deal with it effectively. Being *resilient* is much more helpful that being *perfect*.

To quote a famous Caribbean pirate, "The problem is not the problem. The problem is your attitude about the problem." Captain Jack Sparrow, *Pirates of the Caribbean*.

What do you do on a day when you feel like a five out of ten, or even less? You need a way to bounce back up out of it!

A few years ago, I had a major wobble and lost confidence basically overnight! It was gone. It had leaked out of me somehow. I was distraught and knew I had to do some major rebuilding work, and quickly!

This is where I learnt some helpful techniques, which I'd like to share with you.

I was able to learn this through Cognitive Behavioural Therapy. I am delighted to say that many resources are available on this freely from a variety of sources online.

Here's a summary of what I learnt:

Firstly, it's very important to remember that ***how you feel*** is separate from ***who you are***!

In more responsible jobs you can sometimes lose sight of the person you are, because what you do feels all encompassing. This is especially true in a leadership role.

Sometimes, it is also true that ***how it feels*** is not the same as ***the reality of the situation***.

Being stressed or feeling self-doubt can make fear rule your decision-making. When this happens, you can turn to a reactive approach. This can make you:

- Overheated
- Ill-considered
- Rash
- Fast/rushed
- Accusatory

- Justifying
- Exaggerated

One model of the way the brain processes in this situation is the Red Brain/Blue Brain Model. This model is attributed to Paul Maclean's triune brain theory. I was lucky enough to attend a session with Professor Damian Hughes who taught the model. I can offer a very simplistic introduction to this as follows:

Red Brain is the part of the brain which is governed by being part of a social group. It evolved after the reptilian parts of the brain. So it is more developed than a dinosaur's brain but still fairly primitive. It is known as the Limbic System. There are three main drivers for the Red Brain:

1. Reproduction
2. Survival
3. Belonging to a pack

The significant point here is that when humans feel threatened, they engage *immediately* with this Red Brain. The Red Brain activates the reptilian brain when it receives the threat signals.

The go-to behaviours are to fight, flight or freeze. It is instinctive.

Physiological changes in the body happen immediately, for example, increased heart rate, faster breathing, adrenaline is released. This is all happening to enable the body to react quickly to keep the human alive.

The problem is that the Red Brain cannot distinguish between a threat from thousands of years ago, such as a bear attacking, and something more aligned to our more modern way of life, such as having to present to an audience and feeling threatened with making a bit of an idiot of yourself!

We react the same in the Red Brain and the body.

(Fear featured in an earlier chapter. Threat and fear are in the same category as far as the Red Brain is concerned in this model.)

The Red Brain response happens at a ridiculously fast speed. I heard somewhere that scientists have measured this response and discovered that it takes less than one fifth/sixth the speed of light.

My response to that was to wonder how they could prove it!

Anyway…

The Blue Brain part in this model is governed by the more sophisticated neocortex, which evolved much later. This has two main drivers:

1. Logic – looking for evidence and analysing it
2. The more societal factors – hierarchies, civil behaviour

The neocortex/Blue Brain kicks in about six times slower than the Red Brain.

Interestingly, the Limbic Red Brain does not access the language areas of the brain. That explains why it is so hard to express yourself clearly when you feel afraid or upset.

Responding is much healthier than reacting. Responding is better because it makes you less emotional and more effective.

Responding is BLUE BRAIN. It is:

- Considered
- With breath
- Questioning for evidence

It is a little-known truth that as a human being, with practice, it is possible to be in control of what you think and this leads to having more control over how you feel, which in turn leads to better actions! Some people are better at this than others. You might have noticed this!

A helpful way to think about this in a situation which is making you feel like reacting with your Red Brain is to work through something I call The Helpful Guide. (I have worked through this with many people I have coached, and have only been able to devise this because I went through a really bad patch myself and was totally living in my Red Brain.)

After therapy, I captured what I learnt as follows:

The Helpful Guide

- What am I feeling?
- Pin-point exactly what the feeling is – it's nearly always a fear, but a fear of what *exactly*? (Loss of face? Rejection? Hurting someone's feelings? Getting hurt? Financial loss? Fear of failure? Fear of change? Fear of getting something wrong?)
- Write it down – it's out of your head and on the page (perspective).
- Remember that 'how you feel' is separate from 'who you are'.
- Make some space between the two. Observe your feelings and choose to put some space between who you are and how you feel. Imagine your feelings are the characters in a play on a stage and you the technical director. There are lots of characters that need your attention, but you can CHOOSE (with practice) where to put the spotlight.
- You have a choice – identify which one to deal with first.
- Trace back what you are ***thinking*** to create this ***feeling.***

- Write it down.

- Examine what **evidence** you have to make you think this – **is it truly reliable**? Are you deleting bits of evidence? Distorting the evidence to fit an old pattern of hurt? Are you over emphasising the importance of something before you have established the facts?

- Search for other evidence and other reference points. Who can you ask for a different perspective?

- Ask yourself how helpful is it to think this.

- Ask yourself what could you choose to think which would be more helpful.

- Capture that moment. Write it down.

- Other good questions, especially if we find ourselves in a conflict or having to deal with one:

- What would be an ideal situation for me right now?

- How will I feel about this in an hour's time? Would it be good to wait to see what happens next? What one small step can I take to get a clear head right now?

- Is this something I need support with (e.g. HR department).

- Does this situation require me to keep notes?

- Have I prepared myself for the note taking?

- Have I prepared the other person to be ready to give their side of the story?

- How do I prepare the two sides of the conflict to tell me their position?

- How can I guide each side of this conflict to prepare their position and interests to show the other side? What does that need to look like?

I know what you are thinking now! What has this got to do with a Caravan?

Well this is it:

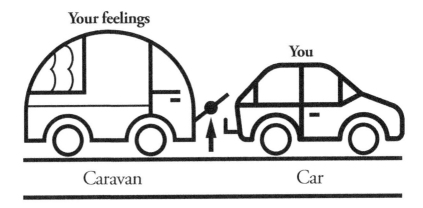

It's a metaphor I devised for the purposes of guiding myself and other people around how they feel. I started it with my boys when they became a bit moody as teenagers, then when I was having a bad day once they told me to unhook the caravan and I felt great about that!

I start using this with a person by asking questions as follows:

Q: What happens to a car when it is towing a caravan?

A: It loses power, it's harder to steer, it is harder to park, it uses more fuel.

Q: What do other road users usually try to do when they are stuck behind a caravan?

A: They try to overtake or get away from it. They get frustrated and annoyed.

Q: What is the thing which keeps the car connected to the caravan?

A: The towbar attachment.

Here comes the breakthrough:

The car represents the true you, your core essence, all your best behaviours.

The caravan represents your feelings.

It is possible to detach a little from the caravan. You can unhook the caravan. Release the attachment.

You can put some space between it and the car.

You can learn to put some space between who you *are* and how you *feel*.

I distinctly remember this when my son Joe was teasing my younger son Luke. Joe had managed to wind Luke up a treat. Luke came storming upstairs in a rage.

I listened to him and I asked him what or how he could help himself feel better.

I said, "Can you become a person who has feelings of anger, instead of being an angry person?"

He said, "How can I do that?"

I said, "Unhook the caravan and put it in the garden and look at it from the kitchen window."

He said, "If I go and play my drums for a bit, I might be able to make that space."

The technique of putting space between who you are and what you feel is easier with practice.

Learning to become the observer of your feelings, rather than being very deeply attached to them takes practice.

The thing which helps most effectively is to take long, slow breaths. Breathe in through the nose for a count of four. Hold for a second or two. Then breathe out through the mouth for a count of seven. Repeat.

The reason our working lives can affect how we feel is because we generally receive a sense of recognition, achievement and praise, plus social belonging and affirmation. These are high level needs which enable us to feel motivated. (Maslow's Hierarchy of Needs, circa 1960.)

During our working lives we fulfil these needs and are able to feel good about ourselves all the time we can '*do a good job*'. Our sense of self and self-worth is affected adversely if the working situation does not allow us to meet these needs.

Therefore, if things at work are not going well it hurts us, because we care about '*doing a good job*'.

It is important to practise the skills of noticing what you are thinking so you can control how you are feeling so you can act effectively. You can choose to respond rather than to react.

You are able to choose what you think to help you feel great about what to do!

It cannot be a coincidence that my life story began with the holiday involving caravans and the breakthrough I had in my life at the time of my father's death uses a metaphor based on a caravan.

Check your pulse

Business leaders can take a leaf from some of the habits of diabetics. They check their blood sugar levels regularly.

Here's why a leader might benefit from checking his or her pulse throughout the day.

As I mentioned, one of my favourite leadership gurus is Dr Tom Barrett. His book *Real Leadership in Real-Time* has been a huge boost to many of my clients working to become successful leaders. One idea from this great book is that checking your pulse will improve your leadership.

Checking your pulse seems like an odd thing to do during a busy day. However, this small addition to your daily routine could bring about a dramatic impact. By doing this you will have learned to pay attention to your own state of being.

Throughout the day our energy fluctuates. Sometimes our personal 'stuff' gets brought into the work we do. This can affect the way we see things, people and the world! Here's what Dr Tom says about a bad day:

"It's OK to have a bad day. It's not OK to manage a bad day badly."

We may think that we can keep the personal stuff out of our working day. Even with our best efforts, there may still be times when it seeps through! Our posture can give it away all too easily. How many of us take time to check our posture? Facial expressions? Gestures? Volume and tone of our voice?

We cannot not communicate. We are transmitting messages even when we don't realise it.

It is usually the case that a family member, PA or close colleague knows what our pulse is doing before we do!

By learning to pay attention to this, you can take action to manage its impact.

The first step is to know your current disposition. This is the easiest part.

How do you feel? Good? Like you have superpowers? Ready to embrace the challenges of the day?

Or do you feel low? Are you ready to fight the day head-on? What if there is a lot of slow traffic on your way to work? How do you feel about it? Is it a chance to sing along to the radio, or does steam burst out of your ears?

By noticing this regularly you can then move to step two to manage the impact.

Step two is the link between your disposition and your level of cautiousness.

Watch out! The better your disposition, the less likely you are to be cautious! This can lead to some dodgy decisions! The wise leader understands his or her disposition and the link to how to get the correct level of caution.

Note: if your disposition is low then you can switch into being overly cautious and miss out on great opportunities.

Finally, there is the skill of understanding the cause of your disposition. Just knowing how you feel (or what your pulse is like) is not enough. It is much more helpful to know why it is so.

Low disposition or mood can be caused by so many factors. Being unwell, having had a row with a loved one, pressure from finances, deadlines, etc. are just a few that come to mind.

Linking back to why you feel 'off' can help with managing how to overcome the limits it puts on your effectiveness. Having a brief moment to notice this and taking responsibility gives you back control.

Great leaders often possess the following superb skills:

- Quick-minded

- Authoritative

- Articulate

All great. However when a small drop of emotion sneaks in, such as anger, and we lose awareness of our state of being, we can easily develop a potent cocktail of what Dr Tom calls 'lethal liabilities'.

Right here is when we should check our pulse. Raise awareness and take responsibility. Try it and see what difference it makes.

Then we can go through *The Helpful Guide* in the previous chapter.

The other thing to mention here is that no one likes or works at their best for/with a moody boss!

People like to know where they stand and don't feel safe in an unpredictable environment.

You are the environment.

Respond consistently in similar situations. That builds trust.

Trust drives everything.

CHAPTER THIRTY-FIVE

BUILDING CONFIDENCE

> "You don't get confidence, you take it."
>
> **— James Vincent, ActionCOACH**

I totally adore James Vincent. He coached me when I spent a year working as an employed coach for ActionCOACH. I learnt an incredible amount from him. He has kindly given me permission to share one of his lessons in this book with you.

Thank you, James. You totally are a legend.

If you, or a member of your team, is struggling with confidence, then you can use this framework to help.

James taught me that at the core of confidence is trust in one's self. If a person is struggling with confidence, the key is to identify which of the seven factors required to build the ability to trust oneself need to be explored.

Confidence is built up *over time*. It can be smashed in an instant!

1. Honesty

This is the first layer in this model of coaching for confidence.

Unless we are honest with ourselves, we can't build confidence. It is the building block/foundation stone.

It might be necessary to delve into the levels of honesty the person in your team has.

What questions would help you discover the levels of honesty about something?

Here are some examples:

- On a scale of 1 to 10, with 10 be total honesty and 1 being not at all honest, where are you now?

- What evidence do you have that you are being completely honest with yourself about … right now, tell me what is on your mind.

- What is another way of looking at this from another perspective, for example how might this level of honesty be visible to someone who knows you really well?

2. Integrity

The next layer is about doing what you say you will do. Not having integrity can eat away at confidence. For example, telling yourself (and others) that you will do something which matters to you or them but not actually doing it can make you feel less worthy. This eats away at confidence as your integrity reduces. It makes you feel like a fraud.

Asking good questions about commitments a person has made and what stopped them doing what they said they would do is key:

- Tell me about what you agreed to do.

- What is stopping you following through on this right now?

- What obstacles are getting in your way?

- How can you reduce the barriers to completing what you have set out in your own plan to do?

- What holds you back?
- What would help you now?
- How can I help to hold you accountable?

3. Authenticity i.e. being true to yourself and your values.

This ingredient of confidence can be about a conflict of values.

It can be about being fake.

It can be about denying your true self to be at the forefront of your daily life – especially at work.

Stopping to reflect on your personal values is important.

Being able to state what your needs and wants are clearly depends on knowing what these are.

You can coach someone to help them be more authentic by having a good understanding of them as a person – your best tool for this is their DISC profile.

Plus having constructive conversations about what is going on inside their head! This relies on a trust-based relationship.

Your job as a manager when coaching someone in this area is to build a good working relationship over time and to provide the space for someone to reflect on their personal values.

Sometimes a job role does not play to someone's best strengths. This requires point 1 – honesty and regular reviews. Someone may feel a lack of authenticity by carrying out a role which does not really suit them.

It's up to you both to navigate this properly with the help of HR.

Ideally you want each person in a role which really lets them shine using their best strengths and to help them develop the skills they need to be able to discuss this comfortably.

How well do you know your team? (DISC)

How effective is the working relationship you have?

4. Resilience

Resilience is the ability to overcome adversity, i.e. how well can a person bounce back after a setback or when facing a challenge.

The best way to coach for resilience is to help a person to plan for scenarios for when things might go wrong so that they have the confidence to bounce back. For difficult situations that a person might face in the job they do, practise going through what might go wrong and create a plan for what to do if these things happen.

Good coaching questions around this include:

- What happened before and how did you manage that?
- What did you learn from the last time this happened that can help you now?
- What skills do you already have that you can use in this situation?
- Who do you know you can trust to help you if this happens?
- What resources are available to help resolve this problem?
- What is the worst that can happen and what is the impact of that to you? To your team? To the company? How can you minimise the risk of this happening? What steps can you take beforehand to reduce the likelihood of this?

5. Persistence

Keeping on keeping on is the best way to build confidence! David Beckham did millions of kicks at goal to be able to 'bend it like Beckham'. He just kept on trying.

It's a key trait of someone who has BUILT UP confidence. They keep trying and that helps them to be able to try new things too.

Coaching around this area can include:

- What experience have you already got of practising this (thing which makes you feel less confident)?

- What helps you to keep going?

- What is the significance to you personally if you keep going and achieve this in the end? How important is that to you right now?

- How will you benefit in the longer term if you keep trying?

- What stops you from wanting to keep trying? (Go to **Resilience** if this shows up as a problem area.)

- What is the consequence for you personally if you don't keep trying? How significant is that?

This highlights the importance of knowing your team so that you can relate to what matters to the person you are coaching.

6. Patience

This is a virtue! Without patience it is easy to give up. It is also easy to be too hard on yourself, which can lead to frustration and negativity.

Learning to be patient with oneself links all the other five factors together.

Your role as a coach is to guide the person you are working with and use evidence to track their progress. This includes holding regular reviews and being a great coach. You have to help that person strike the balance between honesty, persistence and resilience, and being patient.

Great listening skills are key. It is important you are truly present and listen for the clues.

You must also ask great questions.

7. Results

The final layer is examining the evidence of your own activity. Your results are the outcomes you gain from the effort you put in. Tracking your effort and outcomes is crucial. Tracking your own results helps you notice how much your confidence has grown. If you are coaching someone around this topic of confidence then helping your coachee to track progress is key.

Questions to consider are:

- What process do you have for tracking the activity you are doing?
- What are you measuring to see your improvements?
- What do you look for to see how you are doing?
- What does a great day look like? What does it contain?
- How can you monitor what works well or what isn't working?
- What adjustments can you make to ensure your effort brings you the results you are looking for?
- How are you celebrating your successes?
- How do you make sure you learn from the things that don't go well?

Exercise:

If you struggle with confidence, you can practise this approach over time.

Take each element in turn.

If you have a team member who has low confidence you can use this framework alongside the **GROW** Model.

CHAPTER THIRTY-SIX
A LESSON FROM AN EX-VIETNAM PRISONER OF
WAR

What's wrong with you if you rely solely on optimism?

One of my favourite books about expert leadership is Jim Collins' *Good to Great*, there is so much in this masterpiece, but my very favourite section covers the story of a US Vice Admiral's experience as a survivor from the isolation of four years in solitary confinement, as a prisoner of war in Vietnam.

Vice Admiral James Stockdale not only survived his incredible ordeal, he also used it to teach himself something. His survival tactics have been studied by psychologists who study exceptional performance. Of course, this area of study is significant, because if a few people can experience exceptional success or achievements, why can't we all do this?

Collins studied many highly successful companies and compared them to their next best competitors. It was the sequel to his other best-seller *Built to Last*, but should really be read first!

Good to Great looks into those companies who really gained massive traction and powerfully took their results through the roof over a period of about 15 years or less. The factors leading to this success were studied as a piece of empirical research. If you haven't read it, I highly recommend you do. There is much to learn and it contains a few surprises too.

The major piece of learning that comes from the section based on the Vice Admiral's achievements deals with *attitude*. Many gurus cover the topic of a positive attitude and the trait of optimism. James Stockdale revealed a slightly different view. Collins reveals the learning in the section called The Stockdale Paradox.

The Stockdale Paradox emerges from *Good to Great* as a way of looking at positive psychology and adding in another factor: *facing the brutal truth*.

There were many prisoners in the same situation as Stockdale who didn't survive. They based all their survival efforts on being optimistic about their fate and hanging on for the day they would be rescued.

Studies revealed that many died of broken hearts. They hoped for a release at Christmas, then Easter, then in the autumn and so on. Their optimism wasn't enough to keep them alive on its own.

Stockdale, on the other hand, coupled optimism with *facing up to the brutal truth.* Collins claims this as one of the six key concepts in his *Good to Great* Flywheel Model.

Stockdale famously said, "I never doubted not only that I would get out, but also that I would prevail in the end and turn the experience into the defining event of my life, which, in retrospect, I would not trade."

His efforts were channelled into accomplishments to defy the enemy and to take an element of control. He developed a tapping code to communicate with others. He sent a coded message home to his wife, which relayed vital information about the enemy and he used a system of milestones to keep him alive.

Since the study of his ordeal, the Stockdale Paradox has been discussed in leadership circles and it is simply this:

- *You must retain faith that you will prevail in the end, regardless of the difficulties.*

AND at the same time…

- *You must confront the most brutal facts of your current reality, whatever they might be.*

Think back to the previous chapter where I mentioned poor performers.

Some leaders find it hard to admit that they have recruited someone who does not fit with the values of the organisation. It is a classic example of not facing up to the brutal truth. This is particularly hard in family-run businesses. Relatives are often put into roles for convenience, not competence.

Sticking one's head in the sand about cash flow or profitability are two more examples.

Exercise:

Reflect on any 'brutal truths' that need to be faced.

CHAPTER THIRTY-SEVEN
COGNITIVE DISSONANCE AND YOUR
LEADERSHIP

Do you know the kind of situation where you really believe something and you desperately want it to be true? For example, you believe that you are right about something and if it turns out that you were wrong, it would be quite painful?

What if you believed that a person was guilty of something terrible in your company? What if you were sure they had done this dreadful thing? All your instincts told you it was their fault and your belief had caused you to act in a certain way and led you to taking drastic action.

If then you had to go back on this, it could cost you dearly in terms of finance and reputation. Heaven forbid you were wrong.

As a good leader, you would have checked your evidence. You would have been sure to check your facts. Surely you would have not have taken that action if there wasn't the right evidence available. You would be totally in your Blue Brain, wouldn't you?

Sometimes, despite our best endeavours, our brain plays tricks on us when our beliefs are challenged. Our brain tries so hard to uphold our beliefs and can go to extreme lengths to maintain the status quo. Our brains don't like our beliefs being challenged, even when there is undeniable evidence to the contrary.

The study of this human trait is covered by cognitive dissonance theory.

According to **cognitive dissonance theory**, "...there is a tendency for individuals to seek consistency among their cognitions (i.e. beliefs, opinions). When there is an inconsistency between attitudes or behaviours (**dissonance**), something must change to eliminate the **dissonance.**" (Festinger, 2010)

There is a great deal to learn about this, especially as leaders. Important decisions are made all day, every day. All behaviours are based on beliefs and leadership behaviour must be exemplary. You act on what you believe in.

I've been blown away by what the excellent book *Black Box Thinking* by Matthew Syed can teach leaders about cognitive dissonance. I would urge you to check yourself in relation to this. (In fact, I would recommend Syed's book as mandatory for all leaders or potential leaders of the future, such is the importance of the learning contained within, not just this chapter.)

Syed describes, with compelling stories based in research and evidence, just how difficult it is for people to acknowledge when they are wrong.

When Alec Jeffreys had his eureka moment in a research lab in Leicester and realised that it was possible to identify a genetic fingerprint through examining variations of genetic code (and through his subsequent work with Kary Mullins), criminology was revolutionised. Through their work it is possible, under the right conditions, to identify a human being by their unique DNA sequence. The chance of two people having the same DNA code is one in a billion.

This was a major breakthrough. It was suddenly possible to go back and re-examine cases where people had protested their innocence.

The legal system had to stop and rethink previous cases. It was no longer tolerable that an innocent person could be wrongly imprisoned.

Imagine for one moment that you had dedicated hours of your professional life to proving a person was guilty of a horrendous crime. You had found some closure for the victim and their family. You believed you had done all you could to service the community, and had sent the right person to jail.

Then, 16 years later you discover that the evidence could be re-examined with the newly available techniques and the case could have a very different outcome.

Your brain can't compute the extent of the misalignment. Your brain goes into overdrive. You can't bear to be wrong, because it's just too *painful*. For you and for the victim and their family.

Your brain finds ways to align to your beliefs. It goes to extreme lengths.

Matthew Syed writes about the many cases where this has happened and shows us how powerful cognitive dissonance is.

My significant point is that as leaders we need to be aware of cognitive dissonance. We could suffer from it, because we are human, and it's true to say that people we work with, and lead, may experience it too. Understanding it, working on it, using this learning to become a better leader could help.

CONCLUSION
KEY MESSAGES FROM SPEND TIME WITH ME

I truly hope you have enjoyed sharing in my story and my learning experiences. I called this book *Spend Time With Me* because I hoped it would feel like we have spent this time together. The important point is that humans interact with humans all day, every day. Making the person you interact with feel valued is key, especially as a leader AND especially as a parent. Every person is driven by having a sense of worth. Wouldn't it be wonderful if, after an interaction with you, a person feels more worthy.

Trust drives everything. My key messages for leaders are:

- Set out the clearly defined expectations with the acceptable behaviours
- Ensure everyone understands the vision
- Coaching is key
- Questions are paramount
- Effective communication rules
- Listen with your ears, your eyes and your heart
- It's all about the feedback, praise and redirect
- Check and clarify
- Start with the end in mind (Covey)

- Get into your 'Blue Brain'
- Slow is fast with people
- Awareness of self and awareness of others is essential
- Face up to the brutal truth (Collins)
- 'Unhook the caravan', breathe
- Habits, rituals and routines
- Be a bit like David Beckham, it's OK to fail. Use it. Do not apportion blame
- Love what you do
- GROW
- Delegate
- Be grateful
- Spend time with yourself
- Ensure others feel worthy having spent time with you
- Communicate AND connect

I learnt to spend time with me, to listen to my heart and to be grateful for whatever life puts in my path.

I wouldn't be the person I am today if I had experienced a different life.

I am so glad I have learnt so much and I am able to help others learn things too.

I hope this book helps you spend time with yourself, so others enjoy spending time with you.

Now that you have some techniques and lessons about

transformational leadership, I urge you to reflect regularly on your leadership practice.

Here are some reminders to keep you on track:

1. A great habit to cultivate is journalling.

2. When I start coaching with a new client, I always recommend we reflect on what has worked well so far in their business and/or their leadership. Success is never an accident. When something goes well it is leaving clues for you, so take time to notice.

3. If you study success, you will find you create more of it!

4. In addition to reflecting on successes, it is good to be aware that what hurts us most in life is, in many cases, teaching us something.

5. If we get something wrong, or it doesn't go well, then this is a fabulous learning opportunity.

6. A yearly review is a great habit.

7. A better one is a quarterly review because things are much easier to recall.

8. A monthly review is even better!

9. What about taking 15 minutes at the end of each day to reflect on what went well? What about what things you have learnt from? What wasn't so great?

10. If you remember the leadership snippet in Chapter 25 about success, and the fact that the order for happiness and success is that way around (not success first then happiness) then you begin to see that always starting with what has gone well is a huge advantage.

11. Feeling good creates the right chemicals in various areas of the brain so that learning can take place.

12. If you would like to gain an advantage in your leadership, try to remember this snippet: Always focus on what has gone well first in any situation then you can move forward to undertake the learning from everything else. Teaching yourself and your team to always search for the opportunities for learning will build the right atmosphere in your working life and theirs.

13. Having the right support to learn these new habits can be a game changer. If you have never considered leadership coaching before then I urge you to give that a try.

14. Reach out to me to find out about the programmes I offer.

15. I'd love to hear how you have embedded these tips, techniques and theories into your leadership.

16. My other suggestion is for you to delve into some of the great books I've learnt from to gain a deeper insight. The Referencing section contains all of the works I refer to in this book, plus some of the fantastic books I have studied in depth.

    My top four are:

    Blakey, J. 2021. *The Trusted Executive, Nine Leadership Habits that Inspire Results, Relationships and Reputation. Second Edition. New York. Kogan Page 55-58.*

    Collins, J. 2001. *Good to Great: Why Some Companies Make the Leap…While Others Don't.* New York. HarperBusiness.

    Covey, S. 2020. *The Seven Habits of Highly Effective People.* London. Simon & Schuster UK Ltd.

    Hughes, D. Prof. 2016. *Five Steps To Success – The Winning Mindset: What Sport Can Teach Us About Great Leadership.* MacMillan

17. All coaches are leaders, but not all leaders are coaches.

I truly hope you can embed these at least some of these learnings into your leadership practise.

My vision for the future is that leadership throughout the business world will evolve such that all leaders will develop coaching skills. That way all people can realise their full potential because they are being led by transformational leaders.

There is an online course to accompany this book:

Visit:

https://rachelstonecoaching.com/spend-time-with-me/

On completion of the course you can claim two hours coaching with a 50% discount.

ACKNOWLEDGEMENTS

Thank you to my parents for making the person who I am today. Especially Mum, you did a great job! You are a total legend. I love you so much and totally respect how hard life was for you and how much you have achieved.

I am indebted to Neil for putting up with me and being the lovely man you are.

I want to acknowledge my wonderful boys, whom I love so dearly. You have coped so well with everything and achieved such great things, despite my flaws.

Thank you to my lovely brother and his lovely family for being in my life and always caring.

Total respect and appreciation for my dear Uncle Ed for being my safety net and always seeing the funny side.

So much gratitude goes out to my wise guru Graham Davies and your family for allowing me to be part of your lives.

Thank you to Aunty Sandra for keeping the faith. "*This too shall pass!*"

Thank you to Ann and Dave Whitton, and Charlie (RIP Dave & Charlie) for your love.

I could never have made it through without my fabulous friends. I would have faltered so many times. You truly have been there for me. I am so blessed.

Thank you to all my clients for trusting me to help you. You have taught me so much.

To all my employers, managers and colleagues, over the years – I am so grateful for the opportunities and learning experiences. I know I wasn't an easy employee!

Thank you to all my former students. You were such great fun and helped me along my journey.

My local medical centre literally saved me and my family. For all your care and support (Dr McNaughton, Dr Dickens and Dr Hawkins, the MH crisis team and the consultants), I am eternally grateful. Highest respect for the work you do.

Thank you to Discover Your Bounce, my wonderful publishing company, for believing in me.

Thank you to all those excellent authors and experts who have inspired me and taught me, especially Professor Damian Hughes and James Vincent and The Trusted Executive.

REFERENCES AND READING LIST

Acor, S. 2010. *The happiness advantage.* London. Virgin Books.

Adair, J. 1995. *Great leaders.* London. Kogan Page.

Blakey, J. 2021. *The trusted executive, nine leadership habits that inspire results, relationships and reputation. Second Edition. New York. Kogan Page 55-58.*

Bustin, G. 2014. *Accountability: the key to driving a high performance culture.* New York. McGraw Hill.

Collins, J. 2001. *Good to Great: why some companies make the lea …while others don't.* New York. HarperBusiness.

Covey, S. 2020. *The seven habits of highly effective people.* London. Simon & Schuster UK Ltd.

Ditzler, J. 2000. *Your best year yet! a proven method for making the next 12 months the most successful ever.* New York. Warner Books Inc. p103-113.

Evans, H. 2008. *Winning with accountability.* Dallas. Cornerstone Leadership Trust.

Festinger, L. 2010. *The theory of cognitive dissonance.* California. Stanford University Press.

Hughes, D. Prof. 2016. *Five Steps To Success – The Winning Mindset: What Sport Can Teach Us About Great Leadership.* MacMillan

Kennedy, D. 2014. *No b.s. ruthless management of people and profits.* California. Entrepreneur Press.

Lloyd, S. 2001. *Developing positive assertiveness – practical techniques for personal success.* Lond. Crisp Publications.

Portas, M. 2021. *Rebuild: how to thrive in the kindness economy.* London. Penguin Random House.

Sharma, R. 2010. *The leader who had no title*. New York. Free Press.

Syed, M. 2016. *Black box thinking: marginal gains and the secrets of high performance*. Great Britain. John Marray (Publishers).

https://simonsinek.com/golden-circle/

https://www.telegraph.co.uk/news/science/science-news/8316534/Welcome-to-the-information-age-174-newspapers-a-day.html 23.10.2023 *By* Richard Alleyne, February 2011

Ury, W. 2015. *Getting to yes with yourself (& other worthy opponents)*. London. HarperThorsens.

Whitmore, J. 2002. *Coaching for performance: growing people, performance and purpose. third edition*. London. Nicholas Brealey Publishing.

Paul Mclean's triune brain theory

https://www.sciencedirect.com/topics/neuroscience/triune-brain 25th October 2023

ABOUT THE AUTHOR AND
WORK WITH THE AUTHOR

Why Engage a Business & Leadership Coach?
What is the single most important benefit coaching brings to
leaders, owners and their teams?

My favourite quote about what I do as a business coach for my clients is from Johann Gottfried von Herder. He says:

"Without inspiration the best powers of the mind remain dormant. There is a fuel in us that needs to be ignited. Fortunate is the one who has the person with spark around them to ignite their fuel."

Coaching makes you a more effective decision maker as there is accountability – another set of eyes and ears. It forces you to look at your goals and to make sure that everything done in the business is moving you towards achieving those goals. You make time for the really important activities, which leads to success.

What is coaching? Coaching is a process which brings about change for the better. Transformation, innovation, progress, solution, improvement, evolution – all these words can be used to describe change.

All businesses experience change as a constant. By working with a coach, that change is a managed process. Leadership is about change.

I am a leadership coach, which means I work with business owners and key people in the business to support change. This means growing the business, but it is also about change in all its forms. It could refer to a change in personal effectiveness, for example, managing time more effectively or improving work-life balance. It could mean improving profit or something more intangible such as improving team dynamics in your firm. Coaching is a highly motivational experience, which empowers you to realise your maximum potential with dramatic results.

What is coaching *not*? Coaching is not telling or advising.

Working with a coach ensures that you are clear on your goals, directing your activity to achieving them, taking responsibility for your performance and checking in with a supportive person who will ignite your fuel, stretch and challenge you.

Coaching ensures that you raise your awareness and take responsibility for your actions to ensure success. You have a regular check-in and that means you have to focus on what has gone well and what can be learnt if things did not go to plan.

It is highly motivational and has a massive impact on business results.

Having someone to discuss ideas, explore issues from different perspectives and to ask questions helps you really focus on what is important.

This is what working with a coach is like. The questions force you to become aware and to take responsibility, which drives up business performance. It makes you a better leader. It enables you to learn more about running a business as well as having your own set of technical and/or creative skills.

It's fun, tough, stimulating, thought provoking and very effective at helping business owners to raise their game and to achieve more in their business.

Using the wide range of experience, skills and knowledge gained working in management in a variety of sectors, including manufacturing, retail, commercial and education (in both small limited companies and massive PLCs), I set up my own business training and coaching company in 2012. I specialise in management training and business and executive coaching, supporting managers and leaders to develop their skills and coaching business owners to grow their businesses. I work with whole-staff groups or 1:1 with business owners/managers, or the board of directors. I support business owners and leaders to develop improvement of systems and processes and to deploy coaching skills to improve performance. My success relies on building excellent working relationships with people in my network and delivering a high standard of customer service. I am a values-driven, heart-centred coach with a very wide range of skills and expertise. My purpose is to change lives through the skills of coaching.

Most people stay with me for three years on average to prepare their business for sale or to copy the format and start another one, or to pass it on to someone to run so that they can relax with a passive income.

1. Executive Coaching & Leadership Training

I offer 1:1 or group coaching – all programmes are bespoke to your needs. You might want to develop your senior management team's skills or build a middle management team. You might want to set out strategy or to simply set out a plan for growth.

"Start with the end in mind," says Stephen Covey, in his world famous book *Seven Habits of Highly Effective People*.

So, typically we start at the board level to examine the Vision, Mission, Values and Purpose.

When that's all ready, then we go to work to review the systems and processes and identify priorities. This work influences your bespoke training and coaching plan.

To set out objectives for the coaching programme, we check-in with the expected behaviours across the business to ensure that everything is crystal clear.

All business activity is a direct result of the leadership behaviours. We work together to get this right first.

Starting the Programme:

The key decision maker(s) enjoy a **Deep Dive Day** to carry out a needs assessment and agree a programme.

Then we meet regularly (either as a group or as individuals), monthly or fortnightly, depending on your needs, to review progress.

I train the board in the skills of Transformational Leadership and introduce a culture of coaching across the Senior Leadership Team. I then work with, or help to set up, the middle management team. I am also available to support the performance of key members of staff in any way that is required from a coaching perspective.

Programmes are designed specifically for each client, tailored to the needs of the organisation and/or the individual(s).

The investment is reflected in the nature of the programme and is agreed upon following the Deep Dive Day.

The programme investment is paid monthly in advance. There is no tie in, rigid system or schedule, but typically companies work with me for a period of three years, or until everyone in the team is fully competent in their transformational leadership and coaching skills.

Topics typically covered in a bespoke leadership programme might include:

- The art of delegation
- Accountability
- Time management
- Systems and process development
- Appraisal training
- Managing poor performance/providing effective feedback to improve performance
- Communication skills
- Customer service Skills
- Sales training
- Building trust-based relationships
- Setting the values and defining the behaviours
- Skills mapping

2. Public Speaking – Motivational Guest Speaker for Company

Strategy Days

I provide workshops or keynote talks. Examples include:

1. Productivity
2. Inspiration
3. Leadership
4. Time Management
5. Strategic Planning
6. The Power of Values
7. The Kindness Economy
8. Building Confidence

Speaking event investment is negotiated per session/day plus expenses and travel.

Connect with Rachel:

LinkedIn: https://www.linkedin.com/in/rachelstone1/

Podcast: https://www.youtube.com/@rachelstone5880/podcasts

Purchase Rachels' leadership course:

https://rachelstonecoaching.com/spend-time-with-me/

Professor Damian Hughes' podcast:

https://www.thehighperformancepodcast.com/

Printed in Great Britain
by Amazon